BROKEN
Breaking the Silence

Azelene Williams

*Life is full of challenges.
In the end it's getting up that pulls us through the dark days. So that we can admire the sunset
I hope you'll find something special for yourself while reading through my book.
All my love.
Azelene Williams*

Melbourne   New York   London

© 2015 Azelene Williams Revised

All rights reserved. No part of this book may be reproduced stored in a retrieval system or transmitted in any for by any means without the prior written permission of the publisher, except by a reviewer who may quote brief passages in a review to be printed in a newspaper, magazine, or journal.

First Publication 2015 - **ISBN: 978-0-646-94545-3**

Revised Publication 2018 - **ISBN: 978-0-646-98390-5**
Revised Publication 2019 - **ISBN: 978-0-646-98390-5**
Revised Publication 2021 - **ISBN: 978-0-646-98390-5**

Self-published by:	Azelene Williams
Cover Designs by: Williams	Azelene & Sian
Cover Photo Self-portrait by:	Azelene Williams
Back Cover Photo by:	Sian Williams

1st Editor:	**Dorothy Munro**
2nd Editor:	**Janet Vila**

Melbourne　　　New York　　　London

Printed in Australia, the United States of America and the United Kingdom

Azelene regularly leaves her signed books in public spaces around the world with the following message in:

"If you find my book in a public space or if someone gave it to you pass it on, to help me to advocate against Domestic and Family Violence. Read my book, sign it on any page and then leave it in a public space yourself for others to find or pass it on to someone who would do the same.
Putting an end to domestic and family violence is everyone's responsibility."

For a free copy of her E-Book head over to her website:
www.azelenewilliams.com

2020 Westfield Whitford City Local Hero

In 2020 Azelene was chosen by the community as one of the Westfield Whitford Local Heroes, whereafter she received a $10 000 grant towards her domestic violence advocacy. This grant enables her to deliver much needed healthy relationship, consent and coercion programs in schools and the community and allow her to print more of her books like the one you have in your hands right now to handout and leave in the community. She also offered Pro-bono counselling for women and teens in need.

Community Leader

WA Child Safety Services
Creating Safer Communities

www.wachildsafetyservices.com

As a survivor of an intimate partner violence relationship as a teenager, Azelene's ambition is to have a positive impact on today's and future generations. Azelene is a passionate, engaging presenter. She regularly shares her lived experience and theory around domestic and family violence as a founding member of WA Child Safety Services in schools when she delivers the Teen Talk – Healthy Relationships program for Year 8 to Year 12 students. Throughout the sessions, Azelene draws on her personal experience to illustrate the fundamental concepts of unhealthy relationships including gender and social norms, the cycle of abuse, signs of an unhealthy relationship, consent and coercion, the importance of networks and persistence.

> I was really inspired by your story. You are an amazing person and so strong. I was especially inspired when you said that you wouldn't want to do your life over again. So you could help us and protect youth.
> THANK YOU!

> It was good learning these things from some one with actual experience. Usually its coming from some one who thinks the understand it but don't know fully what its like.

Feedback from students: "Thank you so much for educating us with this topic...your real life examples have changed our perspective immensely." "I found out that when you learn something from someone that has experience of what they're talking about they know how to deal with people that are going through the same thing."

Feedback from educators: "Educating our youth early is extremely essential." "Our youth are the future let them grow up with tools to recognise the early signs of domestic and family violence so that they can change the cycle."

I liked it when you told your story. It was very interesting and sad. Maybe tell some more stories about other

I really admire your courage at being able to get up and share your story, and teach people about things like this, which is something we need to know but often don't feel comfortable talking about.

I found Aeelene's story very inspiring and I think that her experiences are something that every youth should be educated about the dangers of unhealthy relationships, grooming and other such subjects. Thank you Aeelene

Thank you so much for educating us with this topic. I have not personally experienced this but your real life examples have changed our perspective emensly.

I think the program is important for youths to learn - knowing a true story of how abuse can affect an individual is important to help educate students.

I loved the story, though it was really inspiring. I liked the videos and how the talk was interactive

BROKEN Breaking the Silence Reviews

Lizelle
"A great, great read. I could not put it down. Finished both your books in one weekend. A fantastic way to spread the word on domestic violence. Azelene, I love your writing style. Thank you for sharing your story."

Belinda
"Azelene, we share a passion for victims of domestic violence. My life motto is Knowledge Is Power. Education is the key. Ladies read the practical and helpful advice in his book before embarking on relationships. Prepare yourself. Don't trust that you will always get it right. Listen to your sixth sense girls and read this book!! Learn what is a healthy relationship. Learn what not to allow and don't become an enabler. Azelene my heart broke reading your story, but I am so proud to know that you have risen above and look at you today!"

Gemma Lawson
"Azelene, thank you for your bravery and honesty in your book "Broken Breaking the Silence". I've had the privilege of meeting you and beautiful Sian, Kidzucate and your campaigns, values and work make a difference to so many lives in so many ways. You're both an inspiration. I've been fortunate not to experience what you have but work with and know of people who have, and it makes me want to help them even more. It takes enormous strength & courage to share your story so thank you on behalf of so many people. You are amazing Azelene!"

Jojo
"In this very well written narrative, BROKEN BREAKING THE SILENCE, Azelene Williams takes us on the road of a beautiful teenage girl caught up in a nightmare with an older young man. She tells us about falling in love and trusting this man who pretended to care for her as much as she cared for him. This is once again proof of how a man can fool a young girl in trusting him blindly, thinking his jealousy is love. Love should be caring, trusting and free of fear. This is a book that every young girl and even older woman should read."

I am dedicating this book to my only Daughter:

Sian Hunter Williams
a.k.a.
My Oxygen

"May you learn from my mistakes, and never ignore the warning signs in an unhealthy relationship. Because before you know it, you will be so deeply entangled in it that there is no way out. I have taught you so many life skills, always keep them close to your heart. You never know when you might need them. Should myself and Dad not be around to support you one day, please find at least one person with whom you can talk to about boy's, sex, porn, politics, religion, guns, tampons, fishing, drugs, wild parties and all the other things we always had open conversations about in our house. Remember, knowledge is key, and asking questions is a part of growing. Never stop learning and experiencing new things. Trust your gut. It is seldom wrong. For the rest, enjoy your life as if tomorrow will be your last day and always remember you make me the happiest person ever. I didn't call you my Oxygen from day one for no reason. There is a lot of meaning into this 6-letter word."

I love you very much
Mom!

"Today I am the mentor, counsellor and social worker I needed as a teenager."

~Azelene Williams~

BROKEN
Breaking the Silence

Azelene Williams

To protect the innocent, some names have been changed!

1st Editor
Dorothy Munro

2nd Editor
Janet Vila

Preface

To my dear readers:

On the 23rd of January 2013 I turned 40 and so much has already happened in the last six months. I launched my 'Breaking the Silence' video today, and suddenly I am overwhelmed with strange feelings. I am also wondering if I have done the right thing to hit the enter button. Do I want to open myself once more to the world and to people who do and do not know me? If this turns out to be a big mistake, I will just need to get over it - fast!

I made the 'Breaking the Silence' YouTube video on impulse: exactly how most things in my life seem to happen. After I completed my Diploma in Holistic Counseling last year, I knew this was important. This was also when I decided to publish my second book, BROKEN Breaking the Silence. While I did my practical, I thought that I would go into fertility counseling. I mean, it made total sense to me. At the end of 2012, I published my first book Infertility: Road to Hell and Back. I believed, because it was a subject that I was very familiar with, that I would end up as a Fertility and

Relationship Counselor. After all, I been there myself and published a book about it.

But surprisingly, a lot of women came to see me with relationship issues, mostly to do with Domestic Violence (DV). In the beginning, I wanted to refer them to somebody else, because it was not my field of expertise. But my clients saw something in me that I had locked away for a very, very long time. It was a dark side of my past that I did not want to revisit or be reminded of ever again.

After one of my clients came to see me one day, I thought long and hard about it. I realized that I had empathy for what she was going through and that it did not distress me as deeply as I thought it would. I was able to push my hurt aside and help her with what she was going through. Suddenly I started to attract more and more clients going through Domestic and Family Violence.

More and more women asking me what grooming was, and why they fell for it. Some women were still caught up in it; others experienced it from childhood or previous relationships and were still struggling to deal with what happened to them. Some were simply not able to break the chain and needed help in moving on. In my heart I knew I was doing the right thing standing up for them, but it was still scary. Did I want people to know what happened to me as a teenager?

After I uploaded the recording on YouTube, I sat frozen for a couple of seconds in my office chair. I stared at my computer screen, as if waiting for an answer. But all I saw was a part of my face staring back at me from the video clip I had just uploaded. It was from the last segment and my face clearly portrayed my emotions.

My left index finger started tapping frantically on the send button, and I realized I was annoyed with myself and tired of waiting. I looked down and softly said, "Just hang on a second. If you do this, there's no turning back".

I looked up again and stared directly into my own green eyes, which begged me to go ahead and send the video - not just for myself, but for women all over the world.

My finger started tapping again, this time eager to back me up and I thought, "For God's sake, go on and do it! What the hell do you have to lose Azelene?"

For a second, I moved forward in my chair, wanting to hear my image on the screen say the words and give me the affirmation I seemed to so desperately need. I stared back and heard myself saying, "Yes! Yes, I have to do this. I have nothing to lose, nothing at all."

Before I could change my mind, I quickly pressed 'send'.

Moments later I realized I had just lifted a huge weight off my shoulders. Finally, I felt free. It was the release of something I had been harboring for years. It was time to tell my story to the world. It was time to break the silence. Sure, I'd 'dealt' with my memories, dark demons and scars, but I always felt there was something more that I had to do. I'd like to believe it was because I never got the opportunity to look my tormentor in the eyes and say to his face, *"Fuck you, you bastard! Look at what you have done to me!"*

What I have learned from our dear friend Facebook is that he has a daughter and that she is the same age now as I was when he started abusing me. Knowing that was heartbreaking and many times I wanted to contact him to ask one question.

"How would you feel if someone did this to your daughter?" But that is something I'll never do. I will never contact him. Not even on the bad days when I have this vast cloud of rage towards him. This hatred has become less intense over the years, but never really disappeared. Now and then it surfaces, and it's at that point when I remind myself that this pain is what made me who I am today. And who I am today is important. I pray that God has protected her and her mother from his evil hands over the years. They say people do change, but sometimes I wonder.

Sliding back in my chair, both my hands fell into my lap, and I felt utterly relieved. I also felt so proud that I was finally speaking out, not just for myself but for all the women who had suffered at the cruel hands of a supposed 'loved one'.

That turned out to be the calm before the storm. Suddenly I was scared to death - not because of what people would say, but because I wasn't sure whether I would be strong enough to walk through the door that I had just opened, a heavy door that I closed many years ago and swore never to open again. Digging through old memories and opening up old wounds. Telling the truth about what happened behind those closed doors, especially the bits that I have never spoken about to anybody, not even my mother or best friend. I was standing at a crossroads and I had to make a decision. I was unsure of what lay ahead, however, one thing I was as sure as hell of, was that I was willing to take the chance to keep doing what I do. Even if it's just to get my voice out there to support other women, women who have been silent for far too long, women who have died because of this silence.

I hope I can offer a glimmer of hope to those who are unable to speak up for themselves, for whatever reason. Perhaps they're trapped out of fear, their predator slowly draining the life out of them, bit by bit, for his own unfathomable, sadistic reasons. Maybe they're ashamed of quietly enduring the pain and degradation instead of reaching out for help sooner.

But, more than anything, I am doing this for my daughter Sian Hunter Williams, also known as 'The Kidzucate Kid' and founder of Kidzucate. God gave me this precious gift, and I'd like to think He had a good reason. With her by my side, I am stronger than ever before. I also have more fight in me now. I had to break those chains of abuse, and in so doing hope to teach my daughter not to make the same mistakes I did. Believe it or not your past has a strange way of playing out in your children's lives. So be careful of the decisions you make in life, they tend to repeat themselves when you least expect it.

If possible, I would like to teach her everything I learned along my life's journey. Most of all I will teach her the power of self-respect, courage and forgiveness. I pray my precious daughter will never have to experience what I did, and it is my responsibility as her mother to speak up and expose my troubled past and hopefully ensure that history does not repeat itself.

There are so many different forms of abuse out there - physical, emotional, social, sexual, verbal and financial - and so many ways that it can delivered including isolation, intimidation, and neglect. These will be discussed in more detail later in this book.

Broken is written to target a couple of things. First of all, for myself, in Breaking the Silence, which is a narrative of my journey as a teenager, caught up in a physically abusive relationship. With telling my story, I will touch on the big question - what is abuse and how did I get caught up in it? I will also focus on the different aspects of abuse. I will talk about why I think women stay with their abusers, specifically in relation to my own experience. I will help identify some of the most common warning signs, as well as offer suggestions on how to get out of a volatile relationship before it's too late.

The last chapter of the book is a workbook, in which I will provide you with some easy to use tools. Using these tools will help you answer unclear questions you may have about your own relationship and help you make confident decisions. You will be able to identify the manipulative techniques abusers often use to keep women within their grasp.

If you feel trapped in an abusive relationship and have picked up this book, it might be because you want answers about why your loved one is behaving the way they are. Or perhaps you're not sure what to do next but know that you need some help and direction before you take that first step. Whatever your reason is, I hope this book gives you the support you need to help you on your journey - not just to heal, but also to understand.

Remember, whatever you do for this person who abuses you, the situation will not change without professional guidance. That is, if he or she is open to change. The issues that formed part of my life during and after this relationship did not just disappear; I had to work on them for a very, very long time.

It's time to take a stand - in your life. I'm sure you know that. All I ask is that you gather your strength, step out of your comfort zone and reach out for help. I know it's scary - I've been there. I know what it feels like to have no idea what lies ahead. If you decide to take this first step with me, I know that you have absolutely nothing to lose and everything to gain. Surely nothing can be as bad as being an emotional and physical punching bag.

I am holding my hand out to help you. Take a firm grasp of this opportunity and together we can help you move forward into a safer, more harmonious place where you can think clearly and make the best decisions for YOU. You might read this and say to yourself, "But I'm not strong enough", "I'll never be able to do it", "I will lose everything", "He will keep the kids" or worst of all "He will kill me or the kids". That's totally normal - it's also part of the brainwashing. Manipulation is key, this is their main intention, and this is exactly how they want you to think and feel without knowing it. What you need to remember is that if you get the right help you will be safe, and you will make it in the end.

You don't have to make any decisions right now. Even if you decide to take no action at all, after reading this book, I hope my journey gives you some insight into what you are experiencing yourself. My only wish is that, my story will help make your pain and sorrow more bearable. Remember you are not alone. Sometimes it brings comfort and courage hearing other people's stories and opinions before taking that first step. Now, let me share my story with you...

CONTENTS

Chapter 1	"All things truly wicked start from innocence" — Ernest Hemingway
Chapter 2	"You'll be surprised what I'm capable of Azelene…"
Chapter 3	It's not what's being said – It's how it's said!
Chapter 4	What is wrong with me?
Chapter 5	Out of sight, out of mind
Chapter 6	Silence can be a killer
Chapter 7	The Show Stopper
Chapter 8	Judgment day
Chapter 9	Lying to yourself is one thing, but lying to your parents is something else
Chapter 10	Kruger National Park
Chapter 11	Olivia Street, Garsfontein
Chapter 12	Close to death, far from dying
Chapter 13	Moving to Francesca "Playing House"
Chapter 14	Eyes wide shut
Chapter 15	Punching bag by day, Hustler by night
Chapter 16	The Dress
Chapter 17	Mickey
Chapter 18	You can call me anytime!
Chapter 19	Do I look like a dog?
Chapter 20	Too close for Comfort
Chapter 21	Present Day

BROKEN

"Breaking the Silence"

Part 1

"I was beautiful the day we met but look at me now. I feel like a dirty old ragdoll, ugly and torn apart. I am broken, and I have questions I cannot answer. Why? Why me?"

It's close to midnight, on a Saturday evening in early January 1993, but instead of revelling in the party atmosphere of the New Year like most 20-year-olds, I am lying completely motionless on the cold, hard floor of my living room.

I can faintly hear the late-night traffic outside the open window of my second-floor apartment facing Pretorius Street in Pretoria, South Africa. Fighting the blackness that threatens to consume me, I try to entertain the thought of calling for help. I know it is pointless.

I lick my lips and recognise the familiar metallic tang of my blood in my mouth. The dark blue carpet in my living room feels like sandpaper under my bruised and battered face. I close my eyes and let a single tear slip down my cheek, leaving a trail of memories and broken promises in its wake.

Lying broken in a fetal position with one eye still closed. My thoughts turn to my mother. Strangely, I wonder what she might be doing. I think about what she would do if she knew what was happening to her daughter right this moment. Would she pick me up and hold me and pacify me like she did when I was little? Would she be disappointed that I didn't recognise the warning signs and ask for help?

Deep down in my heart, I know that she would gently stroke my hair and smile sweetly at me and tell me it was going to be ok - I was going to be ok. With that thought in my mind, a smile flickers across my face, and I feel momentarily at peace.

This mirage of safety is ripped apart when I feel the sharp metal spurs of his boots penetrate the skin on my back.

And I scream, a deep primal continuous scream as he kicks me over and over again - without mercy and remorse.

What have I done to deserve this? How am I going to escape the pure rage and hatred of this man?

My final thought before losing consciousness is the panicked realization that this is the night I am going to die. He is finally going to kill me, and it will be a long, slow, lonely and very painful death.

"Parents can only give good advice or put them on the right paths, but the final forming of a person's character lies in their own hands"

~Anne Frank~

Chapter 1

"All things truly wicked start from innocence" -Ernest Hemingway-

A Couple of Years Earlier.

It was early morning, and I awoke with a jolt to the sound of my persistent, annoying alarm clock. That constant buzzing was the most irritating sound in the world. I hated that damn clock. After promptly switching it off, I lay back on my crisp white sheets and wondered if Mom had remembered to buy me a new one to take with me to Pretoria. Somehow, I knew that if I took that clock with me, it would bring back all the bad memories from school - and that was the last thing I needed.

I had hated school so much. Every single day was like walking straight into hell. I was teased and ridiculed regularly. I had a learning disability and struggled a lot academically, particularly with my reading and writing. Most of the time, I was at the bottom of my class and automatically classified as the dumb, stupid, naughty child.

Nobody except my parents was prepared to go through all the procedures and help they could find in order to make day-to-day life a bit more bearable for me.

A lack of oxygen at birth was the cause of my learning disability. The left side of my brain was underdeveloped. That was the main reason I was right-brain dominant. If you are right-brain dominant, you are normally more visual and tend to process information intuitively as a big picture first, and then look at the detail. You are also more practically orientated than theoretical. The right side of the brain also controls the left side of the body, and most right-brained people are left-handed. I, however, am right-brained and right-handed, although I am ambidextrous with writing.

Year 10 was a total nightmare. Schoolwork was harder, and I knew that I was going to struggle to move up to Years 11 and 12. In South Africa, you need to pass Afrikaans and English to pass your year. I slid on my ass over the years but academically I was going downhill... fast. So, with the blessing of my parents, I decided that the best thing for me was to leave school two years earlier than I was supposed to. I enrolled in a fashion design course at Pretoria College. Attending college was meant to be easier and more practical. I was a very practical person, so this would be perfect for me. As it turned out, I loved every minute of it!

But leaving school two years early came at a price. Growing up in a small town like Meyerton, with a number of families in competition with each other, made it hard for a child like me, especially as my parents were not part of the in-crowd. The biggest challenge for me was keeping my friends. I was not a very popular choice of friend when it came to their mothers and fathers. I still remember my best friend's mom telling her not to hang out with me because I was a bad influence. But that never stopped us, we saw each other often and spent heaps of time together. Fuck - I was only struggling in school, but still I was classified by some of the mothers as a bad influence and a deadbeat. None of them ever saw that I always made sure their kids were ok and safe. I believe that when I left school, the stories that made the rounds went something along the lines of: 'She's a washout that's why she dropped out two years early', or they 'heard that I was pregnant'. Well, I was one of a handful of girls that left school a virgin, so go figure! When I came back after the December holidays with a flat tummy, the stories continued: 'She must have gone for an abortion'. Now, in those days abortion was not legal at all, and the stories were far from the truth. But that's unfortunately what happened in these small one-horse towns in the late 80's. My name came up in lots of household conversations, and I can tell you today, at least I was an exciting subject for the gossipers, by the sounds of things.

The only happy memories I had from school were the times I spent with my friends. I loved my mates and I was lucky enough to be surrounded by them at school and after school. Particularly the boys, as I recall, with a faint smile on my face. I was such a tomboy growing up. I loved interacting with them.

Now, don't get too excited - I don't mean in that way. I always had heaps of boyfriends at school, but they were the kind you could go fishing or motorbike riding with. Sure, I was a tomboy, but I was still a girl at heart, and I wasn't surprised to find myself falling deeply in love with a gorgeous boy named Fabian Rock. If I remember correctly, he was also classified a washout. He was a year or two older than I was, but for some reason he, as well as all the other boys in my school, always saw me as one of the guys and never showed any particular interest in me as a girlfriend. I guess I was happy just being their friend, but in the process, I did miss out on all the schoolyard relationships. In hindsight, I'm not sure if this was a good thing or not.

    I never even kissed a boy properly in my school years...although I did try, once. Fabian Rock, the boy that I liked, came over to my house to watch a movie one balmy Saturday afternoon. We sat very close to each other on the couch and were chatting and laughing about the film, when he suddenly leaned over to kiss me. I don't think our lips even touched when I heard my Dad say:

    "What are you two doing?", as he approached us from the kitchen to ask if we wanted snacks and something to drink. I wanted to kick myself. I was very fond of my Dad, so this was way too damn embarrassing for me to do again, while I was in school and living under his roof. What was I thinking?

    That was the first and last time I ever tried the boyfriend thing. From then on, I was happy to just secretly fall in love with boys that I knew already had girlfriends. That way I would be safe and could just go bike riding with them whenever I wanted, without having to worry about the kissing thing.

In retrospect, my childhood was so uncomplicated. I was carefree and very happy - my home environment was loving and warm, and I was always happy to go home. Naturally my parents had the odd argument now and then, just like every other ordinary couple. I can distinctly remember how awful it was as a youngster to hear them fight. It sounded so scary, but of course everything looks and sounds bigger and more frightening than it is when you're small. But no matter how intense those arguments became; my father was never abusive towards my mother and never raised his hand to her – ever.

As I lay on my bed that morning, surrounded by sixteen years of childhood memories, I realized I was going to miss my family and this home. I'd always considered it my safe haven, and a place where I could openly speak my mind and have honest conversations with my father and mother. I could talk to them about anything and everything, and they always encouraged me to make my own decisions. They trusted me, and I trusted them.

Like most parents, when I made mistakes they were always there to help, and they supported me in my decisions... but they never said, "We told you so".

They gave me the opportunity to be myself, to learn from my mistakes and to form my personality and opinions under their loving guidance and unselfish nurturing. But I felt the time had come to spread my wings, start a new phase in life. I was so excited to finally be on my way to college.

Ronell, my sister, had already moved to Pretoria. She suggested that I stay with her for the first couple of months, until I learnt my way around the city and got used to my new life as a college student. As kids, we used to squabble over everything - perhaps because Ronell was six years older than me, and we didn't have a lot in common. We were very different from a young age.

When I moved in with her, Ronell's husband started his basic training in the army, so having me around for a little company worked out beautifully. I loved living with her and for the first time in our lives, we started bonding with each other. As kids we never really got along. Maybe because of our age gap, I'm not sure. This arrangement also gave me the opportunity to mature and develop outside the safety net of my family home, and it wasn't long before I felt ready to take the next step in my life's journey.

In April 1990, I moved into the city on my own, to live in a private hotel close to the college. At the end of January, I had turned 17, and it was time for me to explore life in the big wide world. It was a daunting, yet thrilling challenge, when my mother and father dropped me off at Majella, a private hotel in Pretoria, the capital of South Africa. Pretoria is 109km from the town I grew up in. I felt so happy to be starting this new phase in my life and knew I had made the right decision to leave school. I was also looking forward to making new friends and proving to myself that I could survive in society. Creating a success of my life was my chance to turn things around.

Most of the work in my fashion design course was practical, so I didn't have the stress of failing. It took me a couple of months to settle and get into a routine, but I soon became friends with some amazing people and loved the life that I had made for myself in the city. I lived to the fullest. Once again, I made male friends, who protected me like a sister and took me with them all over town. My Dad gave me a MINI 1000 that the two of us restored from scratch and painted cherry red. Two of my male friends Andre and Marius also had MINIs, and the three of us would often go racing with them over weekends. Our other friends used to call us Red, Yellow, and Blue.

Unfortunately, one particular morning on my way to my friend's, a bright spark made a U-turn on a one-way street. The car between him and I had just enough time to swerve out of the way, but I was not so lucky. My MINI started to slide out of control and I crashed straight into him.

That was the last of my MINI; it was a complete write-off. Luckily, I walked away with a couple of bruises and bloody knees. My Dad decided not to buy me a car again and told me that my next car would be one I bought myself. He did send me my red scooter all the way from Meyerton, the little town in the Vaal Triangle where I grew up, so I was able to get from point A to point B, and in the end, it wasn't all that bad. Some days I walked to college, it was a good stroll through the city, and I loved to stop at one of the coffee shops along the way, before class. It made me feel so grown up.

Not long after I moved into Majella, a guy that also lived there gave me his pet crab. I named him Rex.

During the warm summer afternoons, I used to take Rex outside onto the patio for a run while I soaked up the sun and read the latest magazine I had bought. At first the owners of the hotel weren't too impressed with me having a crab as a pet. In the end they decided to cut me a bit of slack, when they saw how much entertainment he provided the other guests. Rex would spend most of the afternoons with me on the patio, and at night when I had classes, he would live in the shower in my room. I made him a nice little pad there, and I used the shower in the communal bathrooms down the hall, so as not to disturb him and his habitat. Unfortunately, one weekend when I went home to visit my parents, the girl that was supposed to look after him, forgot to feed him and Rex died from hunger. I was devastated and felt very alone for a long time. He was a great pet - weird, but still a great pet.

Chapter 2

"You'll be surprised what I'm capable of, Azelene........"

Around June that year I met a very handsome, enigmatic guy called Paul, through a friend who was also living at the hotel. Andy was engaged to Paul's sister, a beautiful girl who always looked like she had just stepped out of the pages of a glossy magazine. The whole family obviously had great genes and appeared so 'put together'. I'd never seen an entire family who were so blessed with natural good looks - Paul included, he was tall and gorgeous.

I knew he was out of my league, so I just took to drooling whenever I saw him, visiting Andy. Some afternoons I would even run home from college, so I could sit outside on the patio on the off chance that he might visit that day.

Before you get too judgmental, let's try to remember that I was still a teenager and had only just turned 17 three months earlier that year! I wasn't sure how old Paul was, but I guessed he was in his early 20s. Clearly, my hormones were in full swing and wreaking havoc with my physical and mental state every time I saw this guy. Up until this point I was still a virgin. I knew it was just a teenage crush and kept my feelings for him hidden. I do recall spending many evenings sitting in my bedroom on the window ledge, listening to Roxette and crying my heart out because I missed this man that I didn't even know.

At least my teenage fantasies kept me busy and out of any real trouble. The most drama I encountered was when the hotel manager sent someone to my room to ask me to turn my music down occasionally...

Overall, Majella was a great place to live. Because it was so close to the college, most of its residents were students. In addition to the company of my new friends, it also gave me a delicious plate of food every night. I had my own 4x4m room to relax in, complete with a shower I gave up for Rex for a couple of months, and a basin.

I'd brought a few bits of furniture with me. I had a comfortable mattress on the floor with plenty of scatter cushions, but I didn't have a table or any chairs. The walls were decorated in typical teenage fashion with posters of pop stars like Sinead O' Connor, Madonna, M.C Hammer, UB40 and heaps of photos of my precious school friends.

I had also brought my portable colour TV from home and was lying on my mattress one evening watching movies, when I heard a knock at the door. Evidently the manager couldn't be complaining - I didn't have the volume up that loud...

"It's open," I said casually, lifting my head. The person on the other side either didn't hear me or chose to ignore me, because they knocked again. If it was one of the other boarders I knew they would have just walked in. I wasn't expecting any visitors so, slightly annoyed at the interruption, I rolled my eyes and heaved myself off the bed to open the door.

I was shocked to see Paul standing in my doorway, all 6'6" of him in the flesh and looking divine. I'm sure my gasp was audible. He looked more handsome than ever before, if that was possible, and I had to tilt my head right back to look him in the eyes – wow, he was tall. My mind started to wander before I quickly came to my senses and mumbled, "Um, Andy isn't here. I uh... suppose he's in his room".

"Hello, Azelene. You know it's polite to greet someone before you start talking," Paul said, and gave me a huge grin.

I just stood there stunned and didn't know what to say. That's when he leaned in towards me, and I could faintly smell the fresh scent of his aftershave.
"I'm not here to visit Andy.... I'm here to see you, Azelene," he said, quietly.

My stomach did a complete somersault and every hair on my body stood on end. Me? Why on earth would he come to see me?

Still at a loss for words, I continued to stand there with my mouth hanging open.

"It's also good manners to invite a guest in when you open the door, you know? Aren't you going to invite me in, Azelene?" he asked, with a slight chuckle. I loved the way he said my name.

"You came to see me? Why would you want to see me?" I heard myself ask. As soon as the words came out my mouth I wanted to kick myself, but he just kept his cool and followed me into my room, making a point of slowly closing the door behind him.

Paul stopped in his tracks when he saw my mattress on the floor. I was suddenly aware that this isn't the type of room that you invite such a gorgeous-looking man into, particularly someone who's so far out of your reach.

But it didn't seem to make any difference to him. He just took off his jacket (probably wondering where to put it), placed it neatly on the floor next to the base of my bed and sat down on one of the scatter cushions.

"Well, this is interesting. I like the photos of your friends on the wall. So, what does a guy have to do to get on the Wall of Fame?" he asked with that beautiful smile still on his face, looking me up and down from his position on the floor.

"Nothing really, I can take one of you and add it to my wall as soon as I get the film developed. Is it ok if I take a photo of you?" I asked. There is no way that I wanted this moment to pass. I would love to have his picture on my wall. I took my camera out of my drawer and took a photo. That smile was as beautiful as ever.

"So now I will have to come and see you again to see myself on your Wall of Fame, hey Azelene?" I just smiled and nodded my head like a naughty child. "Aren't you going to sit down?" he asked.

"No thanks, I prefer to stand," I said softly, looking at him. He smiled. I shook my head and realized how stupid that must have sounded. I decided to salvage my response with, "I don't have anything to offer you...to drink I mean?" All my mind could focus on was that this handsome man I had been lusting after was sitting on my bedroom floor!

"Would you like something to drink, Azelene?" He asked and smiled again.

Again, I nodded my head like a small child eager for a treat and, as if he was able to read my mind, he stood up.

"Let's go for a milkshake. That is, if you're ok getting into a car with a man you don't know anything about?"

"I know Andy, Paul. I also know that Andy and Mandy are engaged, so I don't think you'll do me any harm," I said and smiled cheekily.

"You'll be surprised what I am capable of Azelene..." he chuckled softly and raised his eyebrows.
I giggled as he took my hand in his and escorted me out of the room. He opened the passenger door of his white Honda Ballade and I slid into the seat, noting that his aftershave seemed to linger in the car as well.

I inhaled deeply and smiled. I was sitting in Paul's car - how awesome was this? I looked out the window and saw one of my girlfriends peeking from behind her bedroom curtain. I knew that when we got back, all my friends would sit outside on the patio to see what was going on. That was just how they were. They all knew that I thought Paul was good-looking, but they also thought that he was way out of my league. So, what was Mr. Perfect planning with innocent me? What made him decide to visit me and now take me out for a milkshake? The questions flooded my mind, but I decided to push them aside and simply enjoy the moment....

Chapter 3

"It's not what's been said – It's how it was said!"

We drove to Lolly-Pop, a road house not too far from where I lived. I was happy and in my own little heaven. We didn't chat too much while driving. When we got there, Paul leaned over and opened the glove compartment and grabbed a pack of Camel Filter Cigarettes. I opened my door but before I could even swing my legs out, he grabbed my arm.

"Close your door please," he insisted.

I did as he asked and placed my hands in my lap.

"Good girl," he said, without smiling, and released my arm. Climbing out of the car he walked around to open my door. I got out, smiled shyly and thanked him. He never returned the smile, which made me feel a bit uncomfortable.

We sat down, and a waitress strolled over. I wondered what she was thinking, seeing us together. Did she know this was our first date or did she think we were a couple who had known each other for a long time? How did we look together? Paul was head and shoulders taller than me, and he had this aura about him. I don't know what it was, but he was not like any other guy I knew. I ordered a lime milkshake and he ordered vanilla. Paul took the pack of Camel filters out of his pocket and offered me one. I took a cigarette and placed it between my lips. He lit it for me and I inhaled the smoke deep into my lungs, as if I was breathing him into my body along with it. Paul asked me what I usually smoked, and I told him, Vogue.

"You're quite a tough girl Azelene, not many girls enjoy Camel Filter," he said, and smiled.

I didn't answer, but thought to myself, Paul, at this stage I'll smoke tea leaves if that will impress you.

I didn't know a lot about him, so I decided to ask a couple of questions.

"I know that you have a very beautiful sister named Mandy, do you have any other brothers or sisters?" Paul blinked as he took a drag from his cigarette.

"Yes, I have an older brother Danny - Danny Hewson. He's my half-brother."

"Does Danny live with you guys?" I asked. Andy had told me that Mandy and Paul still lived with their parents, but he had never mentioned their brother.

"No, Danny lives with Amy, his wife and their two kids Max and Ben."

He picked up his milkshake and paused to ask me about my family and siblings before taking a sip. I told him that it was only Ronell and myself, that she was six years older than me and married. I also told him about my parents. He asked about my studies and why I had left school. It didn't seem to bother him that I hadn't finished school. I got the idea that he was just curious.

After we finished our milkshakes, he offered me another cigarette and we smoked it in almost complete silence. It felt like ages before he spoke.

"I suppose it's a good time to take you home." I thought to myself, "Not that there is anybody home waiting for me now, is there?" but I decided to keep quiet. I was sure my Dad would be impressed with this man's manners. Taking me home, because it's a good time, wow that's a new one! I smiled at the thought. Anyway, it had been a great afternoon for me. I thought that this would be the first and only date I ever went on with Mr. Perfect. By now he must have realised that we didn't have much in common and that I was just a young girl supposed to be in school, giggling and having fun with her girlfriends.

As we approached Majella I saw my mates sitting on the patio, waiting for me. "I'm going to be the talk of the hotel for the next week or two", I thought. We pulled up to the curb and before Paul had turned off the ignition, I swung my door open and jumped out, the way any excited teenager would do. As I walked around the car I noticed the expression on his face had changed. He held out his hand and I took it. He walked straight to the entrance of the hotel and silently led me into the lift. Without saying anything we stood side by side as it made its way up to my floor. The doors opened, and he waited for me to exit first. I walked out of the lift without looking back. When we got to my room I unlocked the door quickly, but before I could open it Paul grabbed my arm, bent down and whispered firmly in my ear.

"Never, ever embarrass me in front of your friends like that again." He held his grip for a couple of seconds, then slowly lifted his head, looked at me with penetrating eyes and smiled. At first, I was surprised, because I thought he was angry, but then I was relieved to see that he was smiling. I wasn't quite sure what to say, but I did have a funny feeling in the pit of my stomach that was difficult to explain.

"I suggest you get some sleep now Azelene, you have classes tomorrow morning," he said softly. He gave me a kiss on the cheek, turned around and strode off.

Throughout the evening my stomach was full of butterflies and my excitement lasted long after our evening together had ended, and I was lying safe and warm in my bed. It took me ages to fall asleep that night.

The next morning my friends had heaps of questions and I couldn't answer much. I myself was confused and wondered why Paul had decided to come and visit me on that particular day.

When I got home in the afternoon, I found a message on my door from the lady in the office. "Miss Riekert, please come down and see me as soon as you get in." I decided to take the stairs. When I got to the office I saw a huge bunch of red roses at reception.

"Mrs. Botha, you were looking for me?" I asked, peering past the roses.

"Miss Riekert, please remove your flowers from my reception window. I don't get paid to receive your deliveries." I looked at her with shock. "This stupid old woman is one of the rudest people I have ever met", I thought angrily. It was not as though I got flowers every day. I decided she was just pissed off, because they weren't for her.

"Thank you, Mrs. Botha, I appreciate you keeping them here for me while I was in class." I grabbed the roses and ran up the stairs two by two. When I got to my room, I placed the flowers in front of me on the floor. I bent down to smell them. I wished I was able to hug them, they were so beautiful! I opened the card with excitement and read the words in thick black letters out loud.

"Thank you for yesterday, I had a fun time with you...."

There was no name on the card, but I didn't have to guess who these beautiful roses were from. I was so excited, I wanted to run out of my room and shout to the world that I had just got flowers from a certain Mr. Perfect!

"So, this is what it feels like to get flowers from a man you fancy," I said aloud to myself, and smiled.

After that first date, Paul seemed to visit me more frequently than he visited Andy and his sister. We became very close, and I got to know him much better. He made me feel so grown up and always complimented me on the things I said and the clothes I wore. He started sending me flowers more and more often, even though it pissed poor Mrs. Botha off. It seemed the more she got irritated, the more he would send me flowers!

After that first incident I decided never to jump out of the car again. I soon got used to him opening the door for me. Perhaps that was just his way of teaching me how to be more grown up. I would not say we were a couple yet, but I sure enjoyed our 'dates'. It was almost the end of the year, and we hadn't even kissed yet. He was such a gentleman and respected me and who I was. He asked me once if I had ever had sex before and I told him that I was still a virgin.

"Good girl, keep it that way," he said, smiling. That made me feel special and I trusted him even more, because he knew now that I had never slept with anybody and he respected that. Not many guys cared.

Andre was one of those guys. After we had gone out a couple of times when I first arrived in Pretoria, I made it clear that I was not interested in sleeping with him and he dropped me like a hot potato. He only wanted one thing, and that was to get into my pants and I sure as hell wasn't going to let him! I wanted to get involved with a guy who wanted me for who I was and who respected me.

Dear Sian

Always remember there are boys and there are boys.

Some boys will enter your life and will be by your side forever. They will have strong feelings towards you, and their intentions will always be truthful, honest and caring. Make sure you know who these boys are, sometimes they turn out to be life-long friends. Treasure that!

But then some boys will say beautiful things to make you feel good about yourself. Not because they are like the truthful ones. These boys will slowly groom you and use you for their own benefit. The stronger you are, the greater the challenge for them to break you down. These boys also have disrespectful habits and sometimes are called narcissists. They are abusive and don't care about anyone except themselves. These boys will break you down physically and emotionally, and by the time you realise what they are doing it's sometimes too late.

Look out for these boys and look out for their unhealthy behaviours. The problem is when you get involved with these boys you will fall very hard and getting up and out of such relationship is very difficult. If they cross your path at any point in your life, make sure you recognise the signs, pick up the pieces, keep your head high, learn from your mistakes and make sure not to make the same mistakes again and again.

Most importantly never keep quiet. Speak-up and do not allow anyone to mess with your life again. Break the cycle there and then. You only have one life, enjoy it and listen to your instincts.

Not all boys are the same. There are lovely kind males out there. Equipped with the right tools you will find your own Mr. Right.

All my Love Mom
xxx

Chapter 4

"What is wrong with me?"

I woke up one Wednesday morning feeling very ill. I phoned my Mom and told her that I had a severe headache, my eyes were red, and my muscles were feeling very tender. She suggested that I stay in bed. I started getting migraines from a very young age, so we both assumed that it was just a bad migraine attack. She promised me she'd phone the college and explain to them that I wasn't feeling well and that I would not be there today. It wasn't a good time to fall ill because it was close to the end of the year and almost exam time. But the last thing I was going to worry about now, were my studies; I needed to shake this headache.

Just before I had left home my Mom took me to the pharmacy where she bought me three bottles of migraine cocktails. Our pharmacist used to call it his unique combo of migraine killers, and it worked. It was a combination of pills that he would only put together for people that suffered from relentless migraines. It was normally two very strong painkillers, a pill to stop vomiting, a muscle relaxer and last but not least, something that made you very sleepy. It worked like a charm but knocked me out for a day. I took my cocktail of pills and crawled back into bed. I knew I would sleep like a baby in a couple of minutes.

While I was lying on my bed, waiting for sleep to take me away to a place where I could relax and recover from my migraine, I thought of Paul for a second. I hadn't seen him in a week or so, but it didn't bother me that much. The only way he was able to get hold of me was if he phoned when I was at the hotel. The yellow, coin-operated telephone boxes were downstairs and whenever you got a call, Mrs. Botha would answer and then call you over the intercom in your room.

Well, I suppose that she was so fed up with me and my flowers by now, that I would not be surprised if he had phoned, and she just decided to tell him that I was not there. Perhaps because she was too lazy to call me, or just plain spiteful because of her own insecurities? No wonder she didn't have a man in her life. If I didn't know better, I would swear that she took a sip of lemon juice every time I saw her. She always seemed to have this pissed off look on her face. I wonder if she ever even looked at herself in a mirror. Poor woman and the sad thing was that she was not an unattractive woman. She was pretty, pretty with a sour look around her mouth.

Anyway, it wasn't as if Paul and I were an item. We just saw each other every now and then. He in any case had only phoned me once. I still don't really know what he wanted. Because he didn't say anything in particular, and he also didn't call me to arrange a date, or to find out if I was available so that he could pop in. Maybe he just wanted to hear if I was home, because it was a very short chat, a rather uncomfortable brief chat. I was still playing around with the possibilities in my head when suddenly everything faded to black and I was fast asleep.

When I woke up hours later, it was pitch dark in my room. I wondered what the time was. Lifting my head, I almost passed out for a second time. I felt terrible. My migraine had settled a bit, but it was strange that the pills hadn't taken it away completely. I was also very dizzy and felt as if I had been run over by a freight train. I grabbed my watch and realized that it was after eight already. The kitchen was about to close and that meant that I was unable to get dinner. I toyed with the idea of going down to grab a banana or an apple, although I was not very hungry. I flicked my sidelight on and saw a piece of paper on my floor. I picked it up.

"Why are you ignoring me? Why are you not opening your door? Mrs. Botha told me you were here."

Shit! Paul had been here while I was asleep; I must have slept through when he knocked. Damn, and I couldn't even phone him to tell him that I had been sleeping and felt like crap. The house they had moved into did not have a phone yet; hopefully he'd pop in again tomorrow. I wondered what time he was here.

Catching the lift down, because I was not feeling up to taking the stairs, I walked past the entrance to see if there was post in my postbox. I stopped in my tracks when I realised that the white Honda Ballade on the other side of the road was Paul's and that he was sitting in it, staring down Pretorius Street. I jumped at the chance and ran out the door. I assumed he was about to leave and realised I must have just missed him. Pretorius Street was busy, and cars were passing me so fast that my hair blew in my face as I waited for a gap to run across the road.

When I saw my chance, I ran up to the car and banged on the window. That must have shook Paul out of his reverie, because I could have sworn that he got a fright. He opened his door when I moved away and leaped out.

"Where the fuck were you tonight?" he shouted, furiously.

"I was in my room asleep Paul, I came down with a migraine and took some strong pain killers."

"Oh, so that's why you didn't open the door, you were asleep, after drinking pain pills?"

"Yes, I was out for the count. I'm glad I caught you before you left."

"Azelene, I have been sitting in my car for the past 4 hours. I was worried shitless."

"Wow, Paul! Why? What's going on? Why were you so worried about me tonight? I haven't seen you in a while, and that's OK isn't it? Why were you waiting and worried? It's not as if we are going out or anything."

"Yeh, yeh……. I know, it's a bit silly of me but glad you are ok in any case." He replied.

"So, do you want to come in for a coffee?"

"No, I need to get home, I'm leaving early in the morning. I've started a new job in Johannesburg and will be on site for a couple of weeks. I still have a few things to do before I leave."

"Well … ok then."

"Look after yourself Azelene, I'll pop round when I'm back in Pretoria." Paul climbed into his car and took off.

"Weird." I thought to myself. But in a strange way it was a little intoxicating to know that a gorgeous guy like Paul, was a bit obsessed with me.

The next morning, I woke up with a dull, throbbing headache. I still felt like crap! Two days of this was not fun. I phoned my mom and she changed her schedule to fetch me from Pretoria the next day and take me to our family doctor. We walked into Dr. Johan Maree's office and I was flooded with memories. Dr. Maree had been our family doctor for as long as I could remember; I had known him since I was a baby. He took my appendix out a couple of years ago, and he also visited me at home numerous times as a child, when I was sick and feeling too ill to go to his rooms. Dr. Maree was an attractive man with a warm smile. I always felt safe in his company and trusted him as a surgeon.

"I want this girl in the hospital immediately. She's dehydrated, and I suggest we get her on a drip as soon as possible. I also want to run some blood tests to see what's going. I don't feel comfortable sending her home with a handful of meds, before I'm sure what we're dealing with here," he said to my Mom after examining me.

He asked me a bunch of questions, and I answered them as best I could, but at the same time I prayed for it all to stop because my head was spinning, and I was nauseous, and the headaches were getting worse. He made a couple of calls to the local hospital and told my Mom that Vereeniging Hospital would have a bed ready. He gave them instructions to put me on an IV drip as soon as I got there and also to run blood tests and that he would see me in the evening on his hospital rounds.

We left his office just after five, and my Mom suggested taking me straight to the hospital. She would get my clothes later and bring them to me in the evening when she came to visit. Checking in at the hospital seemed to take ages but at last I was tucked in my bed, IV in the arm and ready to get some sleep.

I slept, and slept, and slept for hours! When I eventually woke up, I saw a beautiful bunch of flowers next to my bed with a card.

"Dear Azelene," it read. "I hope you feel better soon. I didn't want to wake you, so I just gave you a kiss goodnight and placed your nighties in the cubby next to your bed. I'll see you in the morning. All my love, your loving Mom." I smiled and felt sad that I had missed her, but at the same time glad that she had let me sleep. I felt a bit better after the painkillers, drip and a healthy dose of sleep. The nurse told me that they gave me strong meds; I suppose that had made me sleepy as well. Dr. Maree knew I suffered from migraines, but I guess he suspected there was more to my headaches than met the eye. I just needed to wait for the results, to find out exactly what was going. We were starting our exams the following week and I hoped that I would be better and ready to go back to college.

"You must have had a good sleep Azelene," Dr. Maree said, early the next morning when he came to visit me.

"Hey, Dr. Maree. Yes, I did have a good sleep. I still feel like crap, but I'm getting there."

"Well, I hope that we'll have your tests back later today. I'll pop in in a while to see if they're here." Time passes very slowly when you're in the hospital. Observing everybody's movements was quite interesting and kept me occupied until my tests arrived at about four, and the nurse said that Dr. Maree would be in to see me just after five.

"Well, Azelene I've got good news and bad news. The good news is, you don't have what I thought you had. The bad news is; I'm keeping you here till I know exactly what's going on with you. Unfortunately, at this stage I can only give you something to control the headaches, not much more than that. The painkillers will also make you a bit drowsy, so I suggest you relax and get as much sleep as possible. I will run a couple more tests as well, in the morning. Let's see how we go with that and then chat again. Would that suit you?" I nodded my head and with that he turned and walked out the room. I gazed after him until he was out of sight. Then I snuggled deep into my bed and pulled the blanket over my head. I started crying and felt very alone. I must have fallen asleep because I don't remember much more than just listening to my own breathing under the blankets.

After ten days in the hospital, headaches that got worse and many blood tests later, my results finally came back and surprise, surprise - I had tick-bite fever! At last Dr. Maree was able to put me on antibiotics to help me recover. The tick-bite fever result explained why my body was in so much pain, why I had the constant headaches and why the migraine meds didn't work. Dr. Maree suggested that I get lots of rest and gave me a letter to say that I would not be able to sit my exams. The college told my Mom that it was ok and that they might be able to use my year's points for my finals. So, the plan now was not to return to Pretoria till after the holidays. I would spend my holiday at home, with my parents and hopefully see some of my old school friends again. I was looking forward to that. It felt really good to be going home. It's funny; I loved living in the city, but at times like these I realised, there was just one place I wanted to be when I was feeling yuck, and that was home, home with my Mom and Dad. That was my safe zone. The one place everything always seemed perfect to me.

Chapter 5

"Out of sight out of mind"

Slowly but surely, I started to feel better. Unfortunately, I got the news that I was not able to finish my year as planned at college, because I missed my final exams, and I had to do the year over. After much consideration, I decided to pull out of the course and take a couple of months off to re-evaluate my life, and what direction I wanted to take from here. My Mom suggested that I help her with her property consulting business, till I had made a decision as to what I wanted to do.

One morning I was sitting in front of the new computer my Dad had bought my Mom, entering all her data for her. She knew nothing about computers, and I had started to use them in college on and off, so I had a better understanding. The program was quite easy, and it was more a case of data capturing than anything else. I was thoroughly engrossed in what I was doing when my Mom came in and asked me to drive through to Vereeniging for her, to drop some documents off at the lawyers for a new house she had just sold. I was happy to grab the opportunity to get out of the office and drive the thirty minutes to Vereeniging. I missed driving so much. This would be a good opportunity for me to think and gather my thoughts. I was suddenly sad that I wasn't as independent as I had been while living on my own in Pretoria, but also happy that I had my family to fall back on. I dropped the documents off and went straight home. When I got closer to the house, I noticed a white Honda Ballade in our driveway. The first thought that popped into my head was Paul. I smiled at that and said to myself, "Don't be silly, what on earth would he be doing in Meyerton?" I hadn't spoken to him since the day he had sat outside the Majella for 4 hours. Furthermore, Paul didn't know where I lived - I had never gone into much detail with him about my life when we did see each other. He was just a fantasy while I lived in Pretoria nothing more, nothing less. We never even kissed, beyond a swift hello and goodbye peck. With that thought I pulled into the driveway, turned the music down and got out of the car.

  To my surprise, as I walked into the house there Paul was sitting in my mother's chair talking on the phone. I looked over at my Mom seated at the other end of her office table, glaring at me with obvious irritation. Paul looked up from the piece of paper he was scribbling some numbers on, babbling out costs to the person on the other end, smiled, and continued his conversation. All I could make out was that he was talking to somebody regarding a job he was working on. Paul was a building contractor, and he tendered for building and revamping jobs at schools across Johannesburg and Pretoria.

The conversation continued for another ten minutes and finished with an evidently irritated, "Well ok if that's how you see it, let's just call it a day and you can finish the job yourself then."

He slammed the phone down and placed his head in his hands, shook it a couple of times, and uttered, "Fuck" out loud. Seconds later he leaned back with a calm, soft look on his face as if nothing had happened.

"Hi Azelene," he said to me. "How're you doing? I hear from your Mom you had a bad run the last couple of weeks and ended up in the hospital. Wow, I'm sorry to hear you were so sick. But really glad that you're feeling better now."

"Hi, Paul, good to see you! Mom, I suppose it's not necessary to introduce you to Paul, as I gather you guys met while I was out?"

"Not really, Azelene, Paul and I haven't exchanged too much. He was on the phone most of the time. If I didn't know better, I would have thought it was his office, and I was the client. If it's ok with you Paul, I would like my chair back so that I can get on with running my business," my Mom said, squeezing out a challenging smile.

"Sure Joan, I'm off in any case now. I just wanted to know if Azelene was free for dinner tonight?" he replied breezily.

"I'm supposed to meet with my modeling agent this evening, but I'm sure I'll be able to cancel it. I would love to go out for dinner," I said, jumping in before my Mom could say anything.

"Great, then I'll pick you up at seven. Sound good to you?"

"Seven will be perfect," I almost squealed. With that, Paul left, and I walked back into my Mom's office. She looked up.

"I don't like that he takes over my office seconds after I meet him. I hope this won't happen again," she muttered.

"Mom, please understand, he works in Johannesburg and his office is in Pretoria. I guess it was quite urgent for him to make the call he did," I protested.

"Azelene, that's not the point. If it was one phone call I could live with it, but he made all his calls from my business phone. I understand that his office is out of town, but I'm not going to finance his business calls. I don't know this man at all. In any case, who is he, and don't you think he's a bit old for you?" My mom replied.

"Well I'm sorry, I don't know what to say, and no, Mom, I don't think that he's too old. Paul is 24 and seven years difference isn't that big a deal is it? You and Dad differ by ten years."

"Azelene all I'm saying is not again, ok?"

I turned around and left my Mom's office.

Chapter 6

"Silence can be a Killer"

Paul arrived at our house at 7pm, dressed in designer jeans and a white T-shirt. He looked as handsome as ever, although I was still very confused about how he got my address and why he wanted to take me out for dinner. I resolved to ask him that evening.
I invited Paul in and asked him to follow me to the living room where my Dad and Mom were sitting having a drink. My Dad stood up to greet him.
"Nice to meet you, Paul," he said, passing him a cold beer.
"Thanks Hannes, likewise. I'm not much of a drinker, but I will have a couple of sips, thanks," Paul smiled. "Thank God he took the beer" I thought to myself. I knew my Dad would have had serious doubts about Paul if he hadn't accepted the beer from him. Not that there was anything wrong with Paul or the fact that he was not a social drinker, but my Dad had always had this crazy idea that men who didn't drink had something to hide, or there was something wrong with them. That was the last thing I wanted him to think or believe about Paul. I was crazy about him and hoped that he would make a good impression on my Dad. It

had been a bit of a shaky meeting with my Mom that afternoon.

My Dad started the conversation by asking Paul about his business. I pottered around the room while they chatted.

"Hannes if you don't mind us leaving, I think we need to go, I don't want to bring your daughter back too late." Paul said.

We left the house and drove to Vereeniging Spur, where he had booked a table for us. The first chance I got, I asked him how he found my address.

"I made it my business to get hold of you. I was quite upset when I got back from Johannesburg to find your room at Majella empty. So, I bought the women downstairs a bunch of roses in exchange for your mother's business name. I remembered you said she had an estate agency in Meyerton. Well, as you know your Mom's business boards are flooding this small town, and by asking around a bit I got her business address. Turns out I was lucky because that's also where you live. Not easy to hide from me young lady, I have contacts everywhere," he replied with a grin.

We chatted about his work, and he told me that he would be working in Vereeniging for the next couple of months. I was very excited and hoped that I would be able to see him more often.

Just before we left the restaurant, I decided to go to the bathroom. When I was done in the cubicle, I walked over to the basins. A beautiful woman entered and looked in my direction. She walked over to the basins and opened the tap, glanced over at me and smiled. I returned her smile and thought to myself, what a nice, friendly woman. She turned away and then suddenly looked at me again, as if she wanted to say something to me, but she didn't. She simply dropped her head down, turned around and left. I thought to myself, "Now that was weird". I could swear she didn't wash her hands. She just opened the tap, closed it again while staring at me, and left. "Strange woman, very strange woman", I thought to myself.

I walked back to the table and looked around to see if I noticed her anywhere. But she was gone. I sat down at the table still looking around trying to locate her in the throng of people, but to no avail. Paul leaned forward and asked what was wrong. I told him about my strange encounter in the bathroom and the eerie feeling it gave me. He laughed and said, "Perhaps she has Alzheimer's and forgot what she wanted to do in the bathroom". I smiled.

"Nope, she's too young for Alzheimer's." We laughed and stood up to walk out.

Paul had parked the car on the other side of the road, and we walked across hand in hand. When we got to the car something told me to turn around. As I did, I saw her again, in a black car right in front of the restaurant. She looked me straight in the eye and started to close her window.

"Paul there she is, the woman from the bathroom!" I exclaimed.

He turned around and spotted her just before she finished closing her window.

"Azelene that's Desi!" Paul said softly.

"Do you know her? Who is Desi?" I asked.

"She's my ex-girlfriend, Azelene. I suggest you stay out of her way if you ever see her again. I heard via the grapevine that she has a new boyfriend. Good luck to him because she's not all there. She has a bit of a reputation. I'm warning you, if you ever see her again stay out of her way she's bad news. She's not the type of person you want to get to know."

I wondered if she wanted to say something to me in the bathroom or if that was just my imagination. But I didn't say anything to Paul.

We got in the car and drove back to the house. He dropped me off just after eleven o'clock that evening.

"Would you like to come in?" I asked.

"No thanks, Azelene. I have a busy day tomorrow, I need to get home."

"Are you driving all the way back to Pretoria tonight?" I asked.

"Nope, I'm sleeping in my grandmother's apartment. She's visiting my father's sister, so her place is free. I'm not working in Johannesburg anymore, or should I say for now. I'm busy with a school in Vereeniging. The phone call I was busy with this afternoon was my client in Johannesburg, claiming he paid me too much for what I had done, and now he doesn't want to pay me anything else, and says I need to finish the job. I told him to finish it himself. I'm not going to stay on a job where I'm not getting paid."

"But didn't you tender on the job?" I asked.

"Fuck Azelene, what's this now, why are you questioning me?" He sounded irritated.

"I'm not questioning you, Paul. I'm just asking, because if you have a contract then he has to pay you what you quoted him for, isn't that right?" I replied, shocked by his reaction.

"I'm not getting into this. You wouldn't understand, you're not in my industry. You get a lot of sharks in the building industry, and clients that don't want to pay. So, I'd rather walk away before I get burnt. Anyway, I have to go now." He got into his car and drove off. I looked at him, wondering why he got so irritated when I asked him a simple question. It was very strange.

I went to bed, but spent hours tossing and turning before I finally fell asleep, exhausted. I struggled to get Desi out of my head. I wondered why they broke up. I wondered what she had wanted to say to me. She was beautiful. She had long dark hair, with deep blue eyes that seemed to be trying to tell me something. But exactly what that was, I didn't know.

Chapter 7

"The Show Stopper"

For as long as I can remember, modeling was part of my life; I loved it, and it came naturally to me. Perhaps it was because of my Dad's modeling career many years ago. My Dad was the first male model in South Africa, and he was popular during his time as a model. He was a very handsome, charming man. So, when I was in primary school, I started modeling and loved every second of it.

I was fortunate enough to work with excellent instructors. Peter van Eck had one of the best modeling schools in Meyerton and the two of us grew very close. I used to go out with him almost every weekend. My Dad didn't mind at all, because he trusted him. He was gay and at that stage in my life my best friend ever. He took me to the most incredible places, and I was always his plus one when he had a function to attend, as he was not seriously involved with anyone.

We were working very hard on an upcoming modeling show and spent lots of time together. Paul didn't like it very much because he often phoned, and I had to say no when he wanted to take me out. But, I wasn't too concerned because we weren't an exclusive item. I was single and only went out with him occasionally.

We had loads of photo sessions before the show. The plan was to exhibit these photos on a big screen, and as we walked out in our outfits, that particular shot would be displayed while we were on the runway. One of our shoots was at a place called 'Fere' in Henley on Klip. It was an enormous success, and the girls had lots of fun. I was especially excited because I couldn't wait to hear what Paul, whom I had invited, thought of the show.

The evening of the fashion show arrived, and everything went well. Nobody screwed up and we all remembered what to do. At the end of the evening we were able to put money on the showstopper - I loved the dress, and my Dad knew it, so he bid on that dress till the very end. When he won the bid, I was ecstatic! It was the most beautiful gown I had ever seen.

After the show, I ran down the steep stairs to meet my parents and Paul. My Dad was so proud of me. He took me in his arms.

"You looked beautiful out there Azelene, absolutely beautiful. You were confident and carried the clothes with style. Well done my angel," he said. My Mom was smiling from ear to ear. I walked over to Paul and hoped that he would greet me with open arms, but as I approached him, he took a step back. I stopped in my tracks.

"Hey, did you enjoy the show?"

"I was disgusted! I feel utterly sick at the thought of you walking around the stage with just a see-through top and panties on. Your nipples were visible and everyone in the room noticed; in the flesh and on the huge projector photo! I'm leaving. This show was one of the worst I've ever seen, utterly tasteless!" He fumed, looking me straight in the eye.

I froze in front of him, in total shock. I felt the tears welling up in my eyes.

"Paul I'm a model, I model clothes and unfortunately, some clothes you have to model without a bra. I spoke to my Dad before the shoot to find out how he felt about it and he told me that if I was comfortable wearing the long black top with only panties, it was ok with him. He told me never to do anything I didn't feel comfortable with, but if it felt good, to follow that passion. So, I followed my instinct and honestly, I felt magnificent tonight. I believe I carried myself with dignity and if I had a choice, I'd wear it again. It's not as though I did a pornographic photo shoot!"

Paul just stared at me for a moment, spun on his heels and left. I stood there sobbing. My Mom saw me and walked over.

"He's jealous Azelene, stop crying and enjoy the after-party. Peter poured you a glass of champagne and he also wanted to have a dance with his number one model," Mom comforted me as I told her what had happened.

I walked over to Peter and he grabbed me and twirled me around.

"Azelene Riekert, you owned that ramp tonight! You were gorgeous. Well done sweetheart. Do you have any idea how far I'm going to take you in your career?

Watch out world, here comes a top model. I'm so proud of you." I felt myself blushing and started laughing.

"Peter, if I didn't know you better I'd think you were the vainest person on the planet! You know as well as I that you would love to be a famous model's agent. And yes, I can imagine what you're going to say now."

"My Bella, darling and what would that be?"

"So, what's going to stop us?" I said, and Peter started laughing uncontrollably.

"You know me so well Azelene, like I've said so many times, if it weren't for my love of men, I would've married you yesterday! Come here you, let's dance the night away. Oh, and your Dad asked me to drop you at home tonight - he said you had a bit of a quarrel with Mr. Handsome. They're not staying late, and I promised to look after his baby girl. So, let's go boogie hot pants - there are heaps of people looking for your signature!" He said with a cheeky grin.

"Ha, ha, ha, you're totally nuts Peter, but that's why I love you. Who's going to make who look good on the dance floor tonight?"

I turned and caught my Mom's eye on the other side of the dance floor, blowing a kiss in my direction. I returned it and then rocked the night away with my best friend in the entire world.

Chapter 8

"Judgment Day"

    I hadn't heard from Paul for a couple of days after the fashion show and spent most of my time helping my Mom with her business.
    I still went to my modeling classes every week but hadn't gone out with Peter for a while. He seemed very preoccupied and busy with his new toddler models. But it didn't bother me in the slightest, because I knew he was just a phone call away.
    One morning however, Peter called me and asked if we could meet. He sounded strange on the phone and I was worried about him, so I asked my Mom if it was ok to leave at eleven that morning to go and see him. I knew something was wrong and that I had to see him as soon as possible.
    When I arrived at his house, he opened the door, grabbed me and started sobbing. I was so confused and just held him for a moment. When he had calmed down a bit I asked him what was wrong. He let me in, explaining that he needed to talk to me. We walked into the kitchen and he made us coffee.

"Azelene I have to tell you something, but first I'd like to ask if you know what HIV is."

I nodded my head and said I had heard of it before. I knew that in May 1986, the International Committee on Taxonomy of Viruses gave HIV (Human Immunodeficiency Virus) its name. I also knew that one of the male hairdressers in town had died of something and clients speculated that AIDS might have been the cause.

"Ok then, now I'll go on. You know Randal, the guy I dated about six months ago for a short period, but it didn't work out between us?"

"Yes, I remember..." I replied.

"Well, Randal phoned me a few weeks ago to tell me that he was diagnosed with HIV. After looking into his sexual activities over the past few years, he discovered that he got it from a guy he used to date. In the meantime, he's been a bit of a slut and slept around with a number of guys, including me. The doctors suggested he phone every guy he'd been intimate with, so they could get tested too. Azelene, I had a blood test done a week ago and they called me at 8 o'clock this morning to tell me my test was ready, and I can fetch the result from the lab. I'm too fucking scared to go on my own and wanted you to go with me. I need somebody to hold my hand." I started laughing and gave him a big hug.

"Peter, Peter, you don't have HIV my friend, you are healthy and beautiful and remember, we still need to conquer the world!"

"Now that's why I phoned you, you always make me laugh and cheer me up when I need it most," Peter smiled.

"That's better, be positive darling, be positive." I replied. Only after I uttered the words did I realize that perhaps 'positive' was not the best word choice under the circumstances. We finished our coffee and made our way to the car.

"Let's drive my car, Peter. I'll be your chaperone today."

"Sounds good to me, Bella," he said and smiled.

The trip to the lab was tense and we didn't exchange many words. When we arrived, I switched the car off and placed my hand on his leg.

"Do you want me to go in with you?" He looked over at me and smiled.

"Well you said you'd be my chaperone, so let's go, beautiful. Let's go and hear what's up with my blood."

We walked hand in hand through the big glass doors of the lab.

"Good morning, may I help you?" The nurse looked friendly and cheerful.

"Yes, I got a call this morning to inform me that my results are back and that I can collect them."

"Sure, what kind of test did we do and what is your name?"

"Peter, Peter van Eck. They ran an HIV test a week ago." She nodded without speaking and grabbed a box out from under the table with white and red envelopes and leafed through them.

"Tell me Mrs. Jenkins do the red envelopes mean a positive result and the white ones a negative?" She gave a soft giggle and looked up.

"No, Mr. van Eck. All our HIV tests come back in a red envelope and the rest in white. It just makes finding the right test a bit easier." As soon as she finished speaking she pulled Peters test out and handed it over. Peter exhaled dramatically.

"Thank God, because if you had handed me this red envelope before I asked my question, I might have fainted on the spot! My first thought would have been, it's Judgment Day, the damn test came back positive."

"No, no Mr. van Eck, please don't worry about that, it's just because of the sorting process that they are all placed in a red envelope, nothing to do with your result, so please don't faint in front of me." We all burst out laughing, and the two of us walked out with a wave.

"Ok, baby, now we have to stop at a bottle store."

"A bottle store?" I asked, raising my eyebrows.

"Yes, it's after 12 and I'm going to celebrate my results with a bottle of wine." I noticed Peter's hand was shaking and I knew he was worried. We climbed into the car and I looked at him.

"Aren't you going to open it?"

"Nope, let's get some wine and go home. I'll open it there."

"Okay Mr. van Eck, let's go." I smiled reassuringly.

We got back to his place and he went to grab a couple of glasses. He placed them in the center of his living room carpet with the bottle of wine between us. He pulled the envelope out of his back pocket and threw it on the floor next to the wine. We both fell on our butts opposite each other. I loved this spot, it was the best place in his house. I loved the longhaired, soft, snow-white carpet. It always felt like I was sitting on a cloud and in winter cuddling up with my best friend in front of the fireplace drinking a bottle of red, was something I would never forget. Unfortunately, that particular day the red envelope that stared at us didn't fit into our regular, relaxing routine. I just wanted him to open it and to get it over and done with. I wanted to get back to our normal routine. I hated this dark cloud hanging over us.

"Peter, please just open it and get it over with!" I begged.

"Later, I'll open it later. Let's drink a glass of red first." We polished off the bottle of red in no time and I decided to go with the flow. "If I'm too drunk to drive home, I'll just sleep over." I thought tipsily. I knew he needed the courage to open the envelope and I also knew he was scared. I didn't want to pressure him and decided to just be there for him. He opened another bottle of wine and picked up the envelope next to the empty bottle. He threw it in my direction and said,

"Open it my Bella." I looked at him and shook my head.

"Peter, I'm not going to open it."

"Azelene, please open it, I'm not able to. You're stronger than I am; please open it."

I held it in my one hand and tapped it with my other hand.

"Peter van Eck I'm telling you now, you're not HIV positive, you're healthy, you're not going to die before you make me a top model and we conquer the world." He smiled and winked at me.

"Then just open it."

I opened the envelope slowly and pulled out his results. I looked up to find his eyes fixed on my face and the tears started flowing down my cheeks. "I'm sorry, Peter, I'm so very, very sorry." He shook his head and said. "No, no, for

God's sake don't tell me I'm going to die. God no! Beautiful, I don't want to die, not now."

I stood up and went to kneel in front of him. I placed my arms around his neck to give him a hug. He pushed me away and shouted, "Stay away from me, stay away! I'm going to kill you; I'm going to kill you! I have a killer virus and I'll infect you!"

"Peter stop." I said calmly "You won't infect me, let's go read up on it first before you push me out of your life." I moved over to him again and grabbed him tight in my arms. Together we cried and cried for hours. After that everything was a bit of a blur, I'm not sure if we passed out crying or because of the wine.

All I remember about that night was that red envelope. To this day I hate red envelopes. What Peter asked me to do that day was one of the hardest things I've ever done! When I look back on it, I find myself thinking, "I know exactly how God is going to feel when Judgment Day comes." It's not easy telling somebody you love, they're going to die - trust me. My friendship with Peter changed irrevocably after he was diagnosed with HIV; he wasn't spontaneous with me anymore; he didn't want to kiss me hello and goodbye anymore; he seldom hugged me. It broke my heart seeing him change so much.

My happy-go-lucky friend slowly disappeared before my eyes. Not long after his results came out he started exhibiting more and more symptoms of the HIV virus. He often said to me his glands were very painful and that he had made the decision not to wait till he got too sick, before he died. He told me that he'd decided to take an overdose of cocaine when he felt that it was his time to go. It made me sad, but I knew he had to figure it out for himself. All I could do was be there for my friend, no matter what. I phoned him a couple of times to find out if I could pop round for a coffee, but he always made an excuse as to why we couldn't have coffee at his place and then he would meet me in town or come over to my parent's place. One day he phoned me and said he wanted to take me out for lunch. We drove to one of the horse ranches and spent the day walking in the fields, chatting, eating and laughing. It almost felt like the old days. He took my hand in his and gave me a big hug.

"Beautiful, thank you for being there for me, I will never forget what you've done for me." He pulled me closer and gave me a kiss on my forehead. I wished that day would never end. I had so much fun with Peter, he was my best friend.

The next week I phoned him a couple of times, but he never answered. That Friday I decided to drive to his house and see what was going on. When I arrived I was shocked to find it empty! Peter had moved out; he moved without telling me! I jumped in the car and drove into town, stopping at all three hair salons and asked the guys there if they knew where he was. They were all shocked to learn he had moved out of his house. I searched for him everywhere, asking around town, but I never found him. I never, ever saw Peter again after that day we went out to the ranch.

    I believe he died shortly after, I think he moved or sold all his things and took the overdose of cocaine he said he was going to take. I think he decided not to tell me because he thought that it would be better for me not to know. Peter didn't have family or other friends that I could phone. I just had to accept it and move on. But I never truly moved on. I still wonder what happened to him. I just hope he died peacefully and not alone.

Chapter 9

"Lying to yourself is one thing, but lying to your parents is something else"

Paul phoned me one Friday morning. He said he needed to go to Pretoria to talk to his parents and wanted to know if I would like to come along. Meyerton is approximately 100km from Pretoria. I didn't have much to do that afternoon, so I told my Mom that I would be going to Pretoria with Paul. He told me he would be at my house around 1pm and if I heard his car I was to come outside, because he wasn't going to come in. He went on to explain that he was in a hurry and needed to get to Pretoria as soon as possible. I promised him I'd be ready.

At exactly 1 o'clock Paul's white Honda Ballade pulled into our driveway. I grabbed my handbag and ran out the house, leaving an "I'll see you later Mom!" behind. I jumped into his car without looking at him, grabbed my safety belt and pulled it over my flat chest. Having no boobs made me look even younger than I was. I flipped my hair back and turned to look at him.

"Hello, Pau... - what the hell happened to you, Paul! Are you ok? What happened? My gosh, it looks like you got run over by a truck!"

"Don't worry - it looks worse than it is," Paul replied calmly. "I went to the Palm Springs site today to pay wages. When I climbed out the car, one of the guys jumped me from behind and tried to grab the money I had in a bank bag. I was holding on so tight, because I knew where this was going. He started punching me in the face and kicking me. He grabbed the bag of money with the wages in it and ran off. I need to get to Pretoria as soon as possible. I need to pay my workers and don't have the money for it. They'll kill me if I don't pay them their weekly salary. I need to go talk to my Dad and see if he can help me figure this out. What I need to ask of you today is, to agree that you were with me when it happened. My Dad's not an easy man and I need to have a solid alibi for what happened on site today."

"So, you want me to lie for you? Did I hear you right?" I asked, looking at him.

"Well I don't see it as a lie Azelene," Paul replied, with a strange look on his face that I'd never seen before. "I see it as protecting myself from what my Dad might do to me. You don't know him. You don't know what he's capable of. You'll meet him today and I promise you, he's not the same person in public as the one you're going to see."

"Paul, I'm sorry, but lying is just not something that comes naturally to me. I was taught not to lie, and this doesn't sit well with me at all".

"You bitch, I thought you loved me," Paul said, staring at me.

"Paul, I do, this just doesn't feel right."

"Whatever, Azelene, whatever."

The rest of the journey was silent. I decided not to ask any more questions and for a moment I wished I had not chosen to go with him to Pretoria. I wanted to meet his parents, but the request for me to lie for him had soured it. I was taught not to lie as a child; this was not how I was brought up.

Paul completely ignored me for the rest of the journey. It was as if I wasn't there at all. The trip to Pretoria felt like hours, but when we took the Waterkloof off-ramp I knew we were not too far from where they lived. I had never been to their house, but I knew Pretoria quite well and I knew they lived in Waterkloof. Waterkloof was not a vast area, but it was one of the top five most sought-after suburbs in Pretoria. Many doctors, lawyers, and other 'well to do' people lived there. The houses were mostly double storey with big lawns. I always got the impression that money was no object in this part of town. I never thought of Paul as wealthy. In fact, I wasn't sure if he was or not. Money had never been an issue in my life. I grew up in a middle-class home and lived a happy life where there was money if we needed it; but we never wasted. Yes, we had our bad months where things were tight, and my Dad hated it if we spent money on things we didn't need, but all in all I grew up being responsible when it came to cash in my pocket and I never took advantage of it. But, I suppose being a property developer placed you in the top earning group of the workforce.

Paul parked the car in the driveway and turned to me.

"You don't have to lie today, but I would like your support in the future. My life can sometimes be very complicated and confusing. There's a lot going on and I need to know that I can trust you and count on you when I need to. Ok?" I just nodded my head. I moved my hand to open the door. Paul pulled it away.

"Don't, that's my job," he said. I felt a bit more relaxed, but still had this bad taste in my mouth over the whole situation. I decided not to fuss about it too much, but I had to pull myself together. We walked up to the house hand in hand and he knocked on the large, solid front door. From the outside, it sounded hollow. I thought to myself, "Today I'm ticking the box that I've walked through the gates of a mansion." The outside light went on, and the sudden brightness caught me by surprise. The door opened, and a tall man stood in the entrance. He stared down at me.

"Now, who do we have here?" I smiled and realised that he hadn't looked at or acknowledged Paul's presence at all.

"Good evening sir, I'm Azelene Riekert, I'm a friend of Paul's."

"Girlfriend you mean!" I heard Paul saying.

"Well, welcome Paul's girlfriend. Come in and make yourself at home." He took my hand and I followed him inside. We walked into a large open area of the house and I realised that this was supposed to be the living area. Strangely enough, there wasn't enough furniture in this room to give it a homey 'family room' feeling; it felt very empty. There were two or three chairs and a couple of scatter cushions on the floor, with a small coffee table in the middle.

"Azelene, unfortunately Paul's Mom and Mandy left and will only be getting back much later tonight. Would you mind waiting here while I talk to my son?"

"Not at all," I said. "I'll be happy to wait here." I looked around to see where Paul was, but he wasn't behind me. I got that funny feeling in the pit of my stomach again. The one I didn't like but wasn't sure what it was trying to tell me either. I went and sat down on one of the cushions and gazed out the window. In the distance I hear a door slam and raised voices. I couldn't make out what was being said, but they were obviously not happy with each other. I wasn't sure if Paul had already mentioned to his father about what had happened on site today. I looked up at the window again and saw a black Rottweiler outside on the grass. I knew they were dangerous dogs if they didn't know you, but this one looked like he was still a puppy. I decided to go outside and play with him while waiting for Paul. I didn't feel comfortable listening to them fight and in any event, I couldn't make out a word they were saying.

I wasn't even outside five minutes when I heard the glass doors open and saw Paul walking towards me.

"What the fuck are you doing here? Didn't my Dad make it clear that you should wait in the living room? Come on, we're leaving." I still wanted to tell him how much I loved their dog and how sweet he was. But there was no time for that.

"I didn't say goodbye to your Dad," was all I managed to say, but Paul just ignored me and kept his grip on my wrist while we walked back to the car. He opened my door, almost pushed me inside and slammed it closed before getting in himself. I looked at him and wondered, "Who the hell is this man sitting next to me?" The next minute he placed his thumb and index finger inside his mouth and pulled out two large pieces of something that looked like cotton wool.

"What the hell is that?" I asked, looking at him in shock.

"There's more than one way to skin a cat, Azelene," Paul laughed. "It's important that I'm always one step ahead of the old bullet. I learned from my Dad, the master himself; now I'm fucking him up in both directions, exactly the way he taught me to do with others. The difference is he's too stupid to realise that I'm now doing it to him. He's getting old; he's not as bright and clued up as he used to be."

"Paul, I don't understand what you are talking about? What have you just pulled out of your mouth? What's going on?"

"Well, let me put it to you this way. I had to pick you up to see your reaction, and to know if my disguise was real enough to fool my Dad. Well it worked and then I played him. I wasn't beaten up on site". Paul laughed and continued. "I just needed some extra cash and I know for a fact that my Dad won't give me any. So, I had to make a plan. You see, Azelene, my Dad is very controlling. He decides who's getting what. I work my ass off and he sits back and decides when I can get a cut or not. Well for the past couple of months it was no deal from his side, so I had to make a plan to get my share of the money. Trust me he's not happy with what happened, but at least he believed me. Fucking idiot!" I shook my head in disbelief. He drove me straight home and told me that things would be very different from now on. He stopped the car and took my hand.

"Azelene I know the trip tonight was a bit uncomfortable for you, but I want you to know that I'm doing this for us. Not just myself, I want you to be part of my life and I want you to trust me. I will never do anything to hurt you or your feelings. Unfortunately, my family life can seem a bit out of control at times, but we won't have to be a part of it forever. I'm trying to get my own home so that I can move out as soon as possible." He pulled me closer and held me tight for a moment. Suddenly I felt safe and happy, in a way. At least I knew that he was trying to make things better. I just didn't like the conflict that much. He told me that he wasn't going to come in and I climbed out and walked inside alone. That evening when I got into bed, I had so many mixed emotions. There was so much that didn't make sense and things I didn't understand, but I tried to block the negative out and focus only on the positive.

The next couple of weeks went by without any issues and I felt jubilant. Paul would come over for barbecues with my family, and we all seemed to get along. My mom was still not very fond of Paul and I now believe that she saw things in his character that she knew were not kosher. But how do you explain to your teenage daughter that her first love is not right for her. Paul and I went out regularly and enjoyed being together. We held hands; we kissed, but he never pressured me into anything that I was not comfortable with.

Sex was never high on my list of things to do when I was growing up. In fact, I got scared even thinking about it. When I was in the first year of high school, my Mom and sister called me in one day and sat me down to have 'the talk'.

"Azelene we'd like to talk to you about sex," my Mom began. Wow, I don't think I'd ever heard my Mom say that word before.

"Ok, so what do you want to know?" I asked. My sister Ronell, who was six years older, looked at me in surprised amusement.

"What do YOU know?" she asked. Now, my parents and my sister may have thought that I was clueless when it came to these things, but what they didn't realise was that kids talk, and they talk about sex, at school. What I didn't know was, we didn't always hear the facts and lots of things we heard from our friends were pure bull dust, but nevertheless we talked.

"Well, what I do know is that a man's penis grows two tiles long when they want to have sex," I replied, looking at Ronell.

"What?" my Mom and Ronell said in unison, almost swallowing their coffee cups.

"Yes, didn't you know that? But what I don't understand is, are we talking about big Italian tiles or small mosaic tiles?"

"Azelene!" my Mom exclaimed. "Where on earth did you hear that?" Now, if I didn't know my Mom so well, I wouldn't have noticed the hysterical laughter in her voice, but I kept a poker face.

"Jacqui told us at school. Her sister has a boyfriend and she told Jacqui". I think my Mom and my sister then realised that they had left the birds and the bees talk way too long!

NOTE TO PARENTS:
Yes, parents - kids talk, and they sometimes talk rubbish it is just the way it is. Talk to your kids about sex and educate them well. Kids are curious and want to learn. Let them learn from you educate them well and truthfully.

A random tip just while I am giving free tips out☺

Be careful of the behaviours you project on your children!
1. STOP screaming at your children! Raising a child this way is NOT helpful. As they grow up, they are going to do the same thing back to you.
2. Don't lie to your kids. They see through you!
3. If you want them to respect and trust you, you need to teach them about respect and trust, and you need to model that daily.
4. Review your own values before criticising their values. They learn most of their values from the people closest to them.

These are 4 of the topics that always come up in my private practice. It's things we should all critically review from time to time when it comes to parenting.

Chapter 10

Kruger National Park

Paul had a friend called Jack, Jack - I really liked him. He was kind and had a great family, especially his mom. She was a lovely lady, and I enjoyed chatting with her when we went to visit. One evening Paul, Andy and I were having a braai (South African version of a barbeque) at Jack house and we came up with the idea to go to the Kruger National Park. It was a spur of the moment decision and there and then we started planning the upcoming long weekend. Jack said that they had a tent we could use and we all agreed to pitch in for food.

A week later the four of us were on our way to the Kruger National Park for the long weekend. The trip started off with a bang and we had a great time on our way down to the park. When we arrived at the camping grounds and took out the tent, we realised that the tent Jack had packed was, in fact, a one-man tent. We rolled on the floor with laughter, it was just too funny. Here we were, four people with one, one-man tent! We decided to sleep under the stars and not worry about the tent. Luckily for us it was summer, and the weather was perfect for a night of star gazing.

We made a huge fire and poured our drinks. Jack kicked it off a bit too fast and was as sick as a dog shortly after the sun set. He crawled into the tent with his head hanging out and started throwing up, making an unholy racket that threatened to disturb the tranquil evening atmosphere. "Keep him quiet," Paul said, "He's roaring like a Lion!" Not realising how loud he had said 'Lion'. The next moment we heard scuffling from the tent next door and people screaming "Lion, Lion, where? Quiet! Listen there's a Lion roaring!" The more Jack vomited the more he made these exceedingly loud roaring noises, and, in the process, the more campers started running around, trying to figure out where the Lion was. It was just too funny, and Paul, Andy and I rolled around the campfire laughing. It was one of those moments, where you had to be there to truly appreciate the humor of the situation. Needless to say, the next morning Jack woke up with a massive hangover and couldn't understand why we burst out laughing when we saw him.

The rest of the long weekend was so much fun; we laughed a lot and enjoyed the time together as friends. We saw so many animals and enjoyed every moment. I remember getting stung by a bee after we were attacked by a swarm. In the process of running away from them, I forgot to grab my mom's binoculars off the table. Needless to say, she wasn't very impressed with me when she discovered the loss of her binoculars, but, shit happens, and I didn't lose them on purpose.

After our return from the Kruger National Park, I had to make some decisions. I wanted to move back to Pretoria to look for work. Paul's contract in Vanderbijlpark was over and he had moved back to his parents. He suggested that I come to Pretoria and live with him for a couple of weeks, to help with his tenders. He was tendering on a number of jobs and he needed some help. I spoke to my Mom and Dad, and they both said they were happy with this arrangement. It made sense for me to be there, if I got to the point where I wanted to go for job interviews. I was thrilled and started packing. At that point, I had not met Paul's Mom yet, but he assured me I would love her and that she couldn't wait to meet me.

I was looking forward to meeting her and spending some time with his family, getting to know them all. At long last things were falling into place for me again and I was able to work on building a future. I was not quite sure what that future would look like, but being an overall positive person, I was eagerly anticipating the new direction life was taking me in. I was able to conquer the world with the support and love of my family, so I was ready to take on any challenge.

Chapter 11

Olivia Street, Garsfontein

"Sometimes the unknown is better for all involved."
~Azelene Williams~

One Friday afternoon at around 2pm Paul picked me up and we made our way through to Pretoria. I was super excited, and I could tell that Paul was also looking forward to this new adventure.

When we entered Pretoria, he took the Garsfontein off-ramp. I asked him where we were going, and he explained that we were on our way to his parent's house. "But they live in Waterkloof, why are you taking this off-ramp?" I asked. He glanced at me for a second and said, "They've moved from Waterkloof to Garsfontein."

"Oh, so they sold the Waterkloof House then"?

Paul replied, "No, they only rented that house. They're renting in Garsfontein now".

"How long did they stay in the house in Waterkloof"? I asked.

"Hell Azelene, what's with all the questions"? Paul snapped.

"Sorry for asking, I'm just making conversation." I mumbled.

I decided to stop asking any more questions. The last thing I wanted was to annoy him.

We stopped in front of the house on Olivia Street and I felt a welcoming atmosphere as soon as we entered the house. Two of the sweetest little boys greeted us at the door.

"Now let me see, you must be Ben and you must be Max." I said with a grin.

They both started giggling and ran off. Next in line was Amy Paul's sister-in-law. She was beautiful and made me feel at home as soon as I walked in.

"Azelene, at last we meet. I've heard so much about you! Don't mind the boys. They're always shy around new people. Trust me they'll be back in the house in a bit and if they get to know you, they won't leave you in peace for a minute".

I laughed, "Hello Amy. I've heard just as much about you and I'm so glad to finally meet you".

She grabbed me by the arm and pulled me into the living area.

"Come, you have to meet Paul's Mom, she's been waiting for you guys to arrive."

As soon as I saw Paul's Mom I knew where he got his good looks. She was one of the most beautiful women I had ever seen. Mandy, Paul's sister, looked just like her. She threw her arms around my neck and said "At last, at last I am meeting the girl who stole my son's heart. Welcome Azelene, I'm so happy to finally meet you. Let's get you sorted my child. We have a full house, so if you don't mind you'll be sharing a room with Mandy. She isn't home often so you won't see her around too much and during the day you'll have the room all to yourself".

I just smiled and nodded. At that point, I didn't mind where I slept, I was just happy to be with Paul and his family.

"Ok, as I mentioned we have a full house. Paul's Dad and I will be occupying the master bedroom. Amy, Danny, and the kids are in the spare bedroom. Mandy and you will be sharing her room and Paul will be sleeping in the office space on a pull-out bed".

"Thank you so much. I appreciate you having me." I smiled gratefully.

The house had the same feel as the one in Waterkloof when it came to furniture. Everything in the house was odd and it seemed as if they were waiting for furniture. Something felt off, but I wasn't sure what it was. I looked outside and spotted the Rottweiler. I asked Paul if I could go say hello. He was a bit bigger now and I wasn't too sure if it was safe. Paul assured me it would be okay, and I went outside. He seemed to remember me, because as soon as I sat down on the grass he was all over me, just so happy to see me. I got the impression he didn't get enough attention, so from that day on I spent some time outside each day playing with him.

At around 5 Paul asked his Mom if he should go buy food for dinner. She said no, she'd made a tuna pie and that we would be eating at around 6. I was ravenous and was looking forward to having dinner with his family. His Dad arrived and soon after Danny, whom I hadn't met before. As soon as Danny walked through the door I felt a dark cloud pass over the house. To this day, I don't know what it was, but there was something about Danny I couldn't place, I just didn't like him. I believe the feeling was mutual, because we never really spoke after our first meeting. When dinnertime arrived, I was relieved. I was so hungry and couldn't wait to get stuck into that tuna pie, I loved tuna! But the first bite was the most disgusting I have ever experienced. It was bitter, and I struggled to swallow it. It tasted as if someone had thrown medicine into it. Strangely enough everyone else ate as if it was the most delicious pie they had ever tasted! After the second bite, I excused myself and went to the toilet where I threw up. I couldn't stand the vile taste of that pie! I went back to the table and excused myself, telling Paul's Mom that I wasn't feeling well and would try to eat something a bit later. The next evening Paul and I went over to the local corner café and bought toasted chicken mayonnaise sandwiches and two 2L Cokes. It appeared that tuna pie was all there was on the menu in this house.

    One evening it would be tuna pie and the next evening toasted chicken mayonnaise sandwiches. The tuna pie always had the same vile taste to it. I still don't know what the hell was in it, but it appeared I was the only one who hated it. I always dished a small portion and took two slices of bread. I would end up eating only the bread. Thank God nobody ever asked me why I wasn't eating the pie.

Every evening after supper we would sit in the living area and Paul's Dad would read to us from the Bible. In the beginning, I loved it because I am a Christian and read the Bible myself. When we sat down to read the Bible, they would have discussions about the things in the Bible that they thought were wrong and were not in line with what they believed. They took things out of the Bible and changed parts of it according to what they wanted to believe. This was very strange to me and I couldn't understand why someone would do that. They also had these recordings they listened to and would use some of the findings from that to change things in the Bible. What they were doing bothered me a lot, because I grew up as a Christian and this did not fit in with my upbringing. I decided to just ignore it and felt that if I did not participate I would be ok. Luckily, nobody ever forced me to take part in their 'home church' evenings. As soon as they started with their ritual after dinner, I would go outside and play with the dog, or sit on the patio reading a magazine. I tried to talk to Paul about what they were doing, but he always got very upset and told me I had no idea about right and wrong and that they were the only people that would be saved one day, because they were following the correct path.

During the day, I would help Paul with the tenders and sometimes he would send me to drop them off in the tender boxes. The day the tenders were read I would join him and it was always very exciting for me. I learned a lot about tendering and working on a site. I also started helping him with the quotes and would phone around for prices. I enjoyed it, and I felt needed.

Going to the schools was great. I think this was the only time I loved going to school. I suppose it was because I was now an outsider just doing measurements for upcoming work. I was not the student getting laughed at because I was at the bottom of the class. I loved seeing the little faces peeking out the windows while we took measurements for new floor tiles or paintwork we were quoting on. I also really liked to spend time with Paul.

We were together 24/7. He was kind and life seemed normal and happy.

There were small things that were not quite the way we did things at home, but I decided to let them go and just try and fit in with him and his family. I was living in their house and the sooner I got with the program the easier it would be for me. It was not as if I had a lot of options.

Mandy and I got along really well. I loved sharing a room with her. She was not there often and when she was home it was for brief periods. Even then she would spend more time in her room than with the rest of the family. Once or twice we ended up on our tummies on the bed chatting away about girlie stuff. Mandy was a real role model. Not just for me, but for others too. She was one of the most beautiful people I had ever met. Well, she and her mother, Melissa. They looked like Jackie Kennedy when she was young. In fact, they were more beautiful than Jackie Kennedy. Mandy's aunt was the owner of a popular modeling school in South Africa and Mandy opened her own Figures Modeling Branch in Pretoria. I loved going to the classes and watching her teach the little ones to model, I mean that was my thing. I loved modeling and was hoping to take it as far as I could. But for now, my modeling was on hold, mainly because of that fateful show that was still a sore point between Paul and me. I got the impression he didn't want to see me on the ramp again.

A couple of months passed, and I was starting to settle in with them and working with Paul, but I knew I would need to make a decision about my life. My Mom and Dad spoke to me often about my future and what I wanted to do, but they never pressured me. Paul didn't pay me, so it was important that I decide what I wanted to do with my life. Was I going to study again or find a job? I think what bothered my parents the most was the fact that I was very young, I was working for Paul full time and didn't get paid a dime. I think they felt that he was taking advantage of me for the wrong reasons and didn't see a future for us, but I was in love and for the moment it was great.

There was, however, one thing that I kept to myself and that was that Paul and I had started sleeping together shortly after my arrival in Pretoria. I was a virgin at 16 and Paul were the first guy I decided to sleep with two and a half months after I turned 17 to be exact. Yes, we had sex for the first time the April I moved to Majella. Apologies mom "I just couldn't start my book with this huge shock in the first two chapters". It was my choice because I gave consent, but it left me really confused and scared because I was underaged. My Mom and I were always very open with each other, but this was one of the things I never wanted to talk to her about, this was part of my private life.

Mothers tend to think they know everything about their kids, but it isn't always true. I didn't believe my Mom had to know the in's and out's of my sex life. I loved him, and I had known him for over a year, so I felt the time was right. What bothered me though, was that every time we had sex Paul would say to me afterwards, "You know this means you are just mine, and no other man will ever want you." In the beginning, I was so stupid and felt good about it, because I felt that I was special. But his comments would get worse and more controlling. When we argued he would say things to the effect that I was cheap and that I had to pull my head in because I would never be able to get a better guy than him.

  He used to say; "No man wants a second-hand girl" This made it personal and hurt me deeply, so I tried my best to avoid arguments. I didn't want him to say these things and I believed him when he did. Sometimes I regretted that I had given him my body but at other times I was ok with it. He was a gentle lover and always made me feel good while having sex. He never hurt me physically and often told me I was beautiful and that he loved to be with me. I consoled myself that that made up for the negative things he would say sometimes. I just had to learn not to be such a bitch and be nice to him, as he used to put it.

  I never told anybody about these fallouts, not my Mom, my sister or my Dad and at that point I didn't have a close friend anymore, so I had to deal with it myself. For many years, I regretted the fact that he was my first sexual partner. I believe the first time you have sex it is supposed to be a good memory. For me, thinking about it puts me in a negative headspace and I then wish I had never slept with him. I also honestly believe I would have got out of this unhealthy relationship sooner if it had not turned sexual. But how was I to know it would turn out like this in the end. I was really young, stupid and in love.

Chapter 12

Close to death, far from dying

*"Life is pleasant. Death is peaceful.
It's the transition that's troublesome"*
~Isaac Asimov~

One afternoon, about six months after I moved in with Paul and his family, I was sitting down with a few things I had to do and had a couple of questions about the upcoming tenders. Paul was looking at the plans and I walked over to him, where he was sitting at the dining room table, and passed him my Filofax to look at the prices I had got for one of the tenders. I wanted him to review them before I entered them into the system. We were a bit under pressure because it had to be submitted in a few days.

Amy came in and said, "Azelene, your Dad's on the phone." I left my Filofax with Paul and walked over to the office area to chat to my Dad. I hadn't spoken to him in weeks.

"Hey Dad, how are you. I miss you."

"Hi Azelene, we're doing fine. I miss you too. How are things your side?"

"Well, I'm learning to do tenders and I go on site quite often with Paul, helping him measure before we do a tender. I'm enjoying it." I replied.

"That's great my girl, but you should think about your future as well. I realise living in Garsfontein without any wheels, it's a bit difficult to get around, so Mom and I have decided to get you a flat in Arcadia and pay for it until you get a job. That way you'll be able to walk to interviews and your scope to find a job will be much bigger. How does that sound to you?"

"Wow, Dad really, my own flat?"

"Yes, you can start looking for a place anytime." He said.

I was ecstatic! My head was spinning and for a second, I pictured myself in my own flat. Oh God, I was so lucky to have a Mom and Dad who supported me, who loved me and who were there when I needed them.

"Do you want to speak to Mom?" Dad asked.

"Uh, Dad no not now, I can't wait to tell Paul the good news, can I phone her later tonight?"

My Dad laughed and said "Sure, give her a call this evening."

"Dad, I love you and thank you SO much!"

"You're welcome my girl, I'm glad we can help you get back on your feet."

I put the phone down and ran to the dining room, grinning from ear to ear.

"Paul, my Dad just called and gave me the best news ever! My parents are getting me a flat, my own flat and I can start looking for one today!"

Paul's eyes filled with rage and he grabbed my Filofax and banged it against his head so hard that the skin above his eyebrow burst open and blood started pouring from the cut, down the side of his face. He threw the Filofax away and jumped up from the dining room table. The chair he was sitting on fell to the side and the plans he was working on flew all over the floor.

"Maria! Maria!" He shouted to the maid who worked for them.

"Where's my Mom's revolver?"

"I don't know." She quavered with wide eyes.

Paul pushed Maria out of the way and ran to his mother's room. I realised that he was totally out of control and that he was serious when he looked me in the eyes and shouted, "I would rather kill you than let you go, where is the fucking revolver!"

With all the commotion going on Amy and the kids came rushing out of their room. I grabbed Ben by the arm, picked Max up and ran out the door, shouting, "Amy get out of the house!" We ran into the garage and I left the kids with Amy so that I could run back inside to get Maria. When I reached the outside wall of the garage, I heard Paul at the window of his mother's bathroom and I stopped dead. Paul's hand was sticking out the window through the burglar bars pointing a .38 special revolver straight at me. The next moment he pulled the trigger and I felt particles of cement from the wall next to my head explode all over my face. The bullet that was supposed to kill me that day penetrated the wall 10 cm from my face. I ducked and ran back into the garage. Ben and Max were hysterical. I told Amy to keep them safe and that I was going to go next door to call the police. My eyes were tearing up and hurting from the particles of cement that were lodged there. My right ear was making a buzzing sound and I was overwhelmed with fear. But I knew I had to stay calm. To this day, I don't know how I held things together.

I had a flashback to April 1988, when I was one of a number of civilians caught in the middle of a bomb blast and remembered rushing out of Sterland just after the explosion and seeing people running in all directions trying to get to safety. No one knew if there was another bomb and then the second one went off. I grabbed my friend's hand and ran down the street. I looked up and saw the Holiday Inn Hotel and knew that I would be safe there and able to call my Mom. Suddenly, here I was a few years on running down the street again. Running around a neighborhood that I didn't know, desperately seeking help.

I was scared to look back in case he was following me, afraid of the next shot. Was he going to get another shot off and if he did, would it hit me in the face this time? I ran past the house next door; it was a corner house, but the entrance was in the next street. I ran around the corner, slipped and fell on the pavement. I got up and bolted to the front door. I banged hard and shouted, "Help, Help, Help!" through my tears.

A woman opened the door and grabbed me by the arm, pulling me into the house. She told me to keep down because somebody was shooting in the neighborhood. I started crying even more and shouted, "He wants to kill me, he was shooting at me!" She grabbed the phone and dialed the police. While keeping a tight hold on me and hiding under the dining room table she told them, "Yes, yes, a child, she's with me, she's from next door. Somebody is trying to kill her. Yes, she's ok but she's scared. I heard the shot, it came from the house next door. Hurry, I'm not sure if he followed her to my house, please hurry! Ok, I'll stay on the line."

She stayed on the phone until the police knocked on her door. All that was going through my mind was "next door, child". I was a teenager but looked so young, even this woman saw me as a child. I might have thought that I was mature, but I was only 18. "Look at me now" I thought, "hiding under a dining room table in somebody else's house, trying to get away from a man who's supposed to love me, but is now trying to kill me." Nothing made sense. Why? My God, what was going on? What just happened? Why did he freak out, what had I done to deserve this? I was only a teen; I was scared and confused.

The woman opened the door when the police arrived and walked out with me. I was crying hysterically. They asked which house it was, and she pointed it out to them. They asked me to come with them, but I was too scared. The one cop said, "Ok we'll go check it out first and then we'll come and get you." They went next door, firearms drawn. It looked like a movie playing out in front of me, but it wasn't, this was real life. I knew how to handle a gun myself. I started target shooting and hunting with my Dad when I was six years old, but suddenly I was shit scared. Maybe because I knew what it was like when you shot something? It doesn't matter how long you hunt, it's never a pleasant feeling to see something dying in front of you. I now knew how the birds and buck that we used to hunt on the farm felt. I'm sure they were just as scared as I was at that point.

A couple of minutes later one of the policeman came back and said it was safe. We walked towards the house and I saw Paul outside on the lawn. The other cop was walking to the police van with a .22 rifle and a .38 special in his hands. He had taken Paul's weapons. Amy and the kids were still sitting in the garage. The officer I was with called to Amy and told her that it was safe and that she could take the kids back into the house. The other cop joined us and said to Paul, "We need to take a statement from you, Paul. Can we do that inside?" Paul nodded and waved them in. I walked between him and the cops and just before we got to the door, I felt a fist in my back. Paul shoved me from behind, so hard that I fell into the flowerbed next to the front door. As I hit the ground the cops turned around and Paul bent down to help me up saying, "Are you ok? She fell". I thought to myself "You asshole; yes I fell, because you fucking punched me with a fist between my shoulder blades! You knocked me to the ground. Who are you, you sick psycho?" The one officer walked me through the house to the outside area at the back, where he took my statement. The other one stayed inside the house with Paul. Amy and the kids were nowhere to be seen. In the distance, I could hear Max crying somewhere. The statement took about an hour. The officer that took Paul's statement came outside and asked if I wanted to phone someone. He said he didn't think it was a good idea for me to stay at the house. He suggested I call someone while they spoke to Maria and Amy.

I phoned Ronell and told her what had happened and that I needed her to come fetch me. She was there in less than half an hour. We left Paul's house while the cops were still there, and Ronell turned to me and said, "I know what you need. You need a stiff drink." The two of us drove to Hatfield and ended up talking late into the evening. I didn't tell her about all our issues, just about the day's happenings. By the time we got back to her house, I was more than a little tipsy. As we turned into the driveway, I heard her say,

"Azelene, look up." I lifted my head and saw hundreds of red roses scattered over the drive, leading to her front door. I knew this was Paul's handy work. We got out of the car and I started picking the long-stemmed roses up. I didn't see his Honda parked on the other side of the road. The next moment, I saw his headlights as he drove in and stopped behind Ronell's car.

He climbed out and started crying like a baby. I could see the pain on his face as he pleaded with me to come home with him. He was shaking and looked so pathetic there in the moonlight, the tears streaming down his face. Now I can't even remember all the lame excuses he came up with, as to why he pulled the trigger on me just hours earlier. But what he said worked, because under a half hour later I was in his car, driving back to his parent's house. I have a mental block about what happened over the next couple of days, until the weekend when my parents came through from Meyerton for a meeting with Paul's parents, Paul, Ronell and I, at my sister's house. What was said in that meeting is also a bit of a blur to me, but I do remember

Paul taking the bible out, talking, praying and he even had my Dad in tears! My Dad was a tough guy; he didn't cry easily.

In fact, I do believe that was the first and only time I ever saw my father in tears. My Mom kept a stony face. She had her own issues with Paul and nothing he said or did persuaded her in any way to believe in his innocence. Ronell also had a huge problem with him, I think she saw straight through him. After a lot of talking, pleading, praying and crying from Paul's side, I left with him and his parents. I stayed another couple of weeks with them. Not long after, my Dad contacted me to tell me that he had found me a flat and that I'd be moving in at the end of the month. Paul handled the situation much better this time and it all suddenly seemed normal again. He played the 'good boy' card and at times it felt as if nothing bad had happened. But I was wary, scared to trigger anything. We didn't go out much and spent most of our time with his family, just lying around the house.

In a way, it was good because I felt safe with his parents around, but I also wished that we were a bit more social. I missed my friends and the fun barbeques and parties we used to have. At times, I missed my Majella days and the friends I had made there. I was very popular and had a lot of friends. I often wondered how my life would have turned out if I had gone back to college and completed my fashion design course.

I was also really missing my modeling career. I loved being in front of the camera and had worked with amazing people and made good friends that I didn't see any more. In a way, I felt isolated, even though I was with the man I loved. Was this love or was it confusion? Was I old enough to make adult decisions? Was I old enough the day I left home? Looking back, I don't believe I was, but would I have listened if my parents had tried to force me to do what they wanted me to? I highly doubt it.

Chapter 13

Moving to Francesca "Playing House"

"And the danger is that in this move toward new horizons and far directions that I may lose what I have now, and not find anything except loneliness."
-Sylvia Plath-

My Dad loved working with his hands. He was a handyman like no other, always busy building or fixing something. He also made the most beautiful wrought iron furniture in his spare time. When I moved to Francesca, my Dad took the opportunity to make the furniture for my bedroom and lounge.

It was a small bachelor flat with a kitchen, bathroom, lounge and balcony bedroom, but it was perfect for me. Paul started a job in Johannesburg and I had a bit of space; breathing space. I enjoyed the time with my Mom and Dad, working to set my new home up. In the coming weeks, Ronell organised a position for me at an anesthesiologist at Meulmed Hospital, just a block from where I was living. Everything seemed to be falling into place. I had my own little pad now and was able to live my life and grow up. I was young, but I knew that I'd be ok. I had overcome so much since my school days and taking on this new challenge seemed easy and felt like lots of fun. I couldn't wait for my parents to leave, so I could start playing house.

Paul began coming over on weekends and slept over when he was in Pretoria. But, soon after his job in Johannesburg was finished, he moved in with me. We spent a lot of time together and I missed my space, but it was great to have him around. A couple of months after I moved in, we were invited to go on holiday with Ronell and Stefan. I was stoked! We went down to the KwaZulu-Natal coast.

The first part of the week was great but, one day on the beach things turned sour. We were playing volleyball on the beach, having fun. Without warning, I got a fist in the side of my ribs. I fell, and Paul acted as if it was an accident. I knew it wasn't. This kind of thing was happening far too often and in hindsight I realise that there was a pattern, but back then I was just shocked, hurt and confused.

Strangely enough, he picked public places to get a punch in here or there. Specifically, because he knew that I would not react in front of people and he got away with it by pretending it was an accident. It was also an easy way for me to explain the bruises. These 'accidents' happened so often in public that the marks that started to appear at home, when he grabbed me or punched me once or twice out of frustration, were brushed off as nothing.

This was the same behavior that he displayed the day of the shooting, when he planted a fist in my back right in front of the police officers and then pretended that I had lost my balance and tripped. I was so angry with him then and I was angry now too. The next day we were out on the beach playing volleyball again. This time I was brought to the ground with a fist in my stomach, also 'by accident'. I then had sand kicked in my face as he pulled me to my feet. I knew that none of this was accidental. I also knew that, while the atmosphere was dampened by my mood, his attitude made it much worse, because he said that I couldn't handle the game. He blamed me for what happened and became so angry that he wanted to go home by train immediately.

I knew that I had to calm him down because there was no way that I wanted to catch a train back to Pretoria alone with this man. He wouldn't just leave it there. I was terrified of what he might do to me when we got home, or even worse – while we were still on the train. Ronell and Stefan would not go back with us if we decided to leave now.

The rest of the holiday was a blur, apart from when Ronell had a reaction to iodine, after eating seafood, and was rushed to the hospital because her face had doubled in size and she couldn't breathe. She received injections at the emergency room and looked and felt much better the next day.

I think Ronell and Stefan picked up on the tension between Paul and I, so getting back to Pretoria was a relief at the end of the day. By the time we returned, things were a bit more relaxed between us.

Paul didn't take the things that happened on holiday out on me and returning to work the following week was more relaxing than the holiday had been. I was happy to get back to my routine. Ronell and I never talked about the holiday and she never asked me what was going on between Paul and me. She respected my privacy and I respected hers.

Chapter 14

Eyes wide shut!!!

Usually, as soon as I realised I was awake, I opened my eyes and got out of bed. But on this particular morning I felt quite happy when I woke up and so I kept my eyes closed for a moment.

Have you ever noticed that when you think back on the morning, you're not able to remember if you opened your eyes as soon as your brain said it was time to get up? Well, I started to get into a routine of not opening my eyes before I was ready and willing to face the man lying next to me. I would retreat to my happy place as soon as I woke up, with my eyes still closed. That was my only escape from reality. Facing the fact that I was living in the middle of a real-life nightmare was frightening.

A nightmare I didn't know how to get out of and one where I had started to fear for my life. I had kept quiet for so long by then, that I got to the point where I was not sure what I believed and what I knew was real. I was so confused by the many mind games that Paul had played on me. I knew that this was not a good situation and I knew that I was not happy with where I was, but I had no idea how to get out of it. I was imprisoned in this life, because I had got used to being his punching bag. I was used to being nothing more than an object for him to take his anger and frustration out on, because I became convinced that no one else would want me anymore.

The saddest part is, I was totally alone. There was no way on earth that I would be able to share this with anyone. I was living a lie. Not just lying to myself but to every damn person that knew me. Or dare I say - used to know me. I looked at my life and saw no one. Less than two years ago I had many friends; friends I loved and that loved and respected me. Now I was lying here next to a monster and I was too scared to open my eyes, because if he knew that I was awake all hell would break loose. The verbal abuse would start and maybe, just maybe, if I was lucky, I would be quick enough to dodge a slap. As long as my eyes were closed, I could be me, dream about myself in my happy, carefree world. I just needed to be careful not to smile.

I felt him move next to me and wasn't sure if he was awake. I was not going to peek to see if he was. I was just going to stay here where I was for now; here where I could be who I wanted, with whom I wanted and wherever I wanted.

"What is it with the smirk on your face Azelene? Are you dreaming or are you awake?"

"Fuck," I thought to myself, "I smiled, I wasn't supposed to smile! I was smiling inwardly; I didn't realise that I had inadvertently let it show on my face!"

I had to do something; I had to think fast. I stretched out and gave a big yawn.

"Good morning," I smiled.

"What the fuck were you smiling about?" Paul looked at me, clearly pissed off.

"Smiling, me? Not quite sure, I must have been dreaming." I replied, hesitantly.

"Dreaming, so what have you been dreaming about?" He asked, suspiciously.

"I don't know Paul; I can't remember."

WHACK! His hand connected with my face.

"If I find out that you're lying to me you'll get more than just a slap on the cheek. Are you seeing somebody?"

I felt a warm tear rolling down my face but before I could reply, he continued, "Stop being such a sissy, I haven't even touched you. Wait till I really slap you, then you'll have a good reason to cry."

For a moment I wondered if this was what his parents used to say to him as a child. This rage had to come from somewhere. But then again, if I looked at the picture-perfect family, it was difficult to believe that such cruel, distrustful aggression could be part of their history. Here was the perfect looking man in front of me, with such a violent and abusive nature.

I couldn't understand it; I didn't understand it at all. I rolled onto my other side to get him out of my peripheral vision.

"This is not how I want to wake up on a Saturday morning Paul," I said quietly.

"Well stop being such a bitch then and stop lying. You're doing this to yourself, nobody else is to blame," I heard him hiss.

What was wrong with me? If I had just opened my eyes when I realised that I was awake, none of this would have happened.

Paul was right, what happened this morning was all my own fault. I was such a bitch. As I looked at myself in the bathroom mirror, I was still able to see his finger marks on my cheek. It was a good thing I was getting used to wearing more make-up. I couldn't leave the flat with this puffy red cheek. Thank God I didn't have to work today, I was slowly running out of excuses. I was sure Ronell was going to smell a rat about my constant bruises. Up until now I had been able to hide them and the few times it was noticeable, I was able to elaborate and come up with a good story. I was sure she believed me when I went to work with a black eye. These things happened. People hurt themselves, fell and stumbled into doors. I just needed to believe it myself and believe that I deserved it, like this morning's slap. It couldn't get worse than this, could it?

"So, are you going to tell me what or who your dream was about?" He was standing in the doorway staring at me as I lay soaking in the warm bath he had made for me as an apology, replete with bubbles and dried rose petals. I wanted to slide down into the water and drown myself, but I refused to draw my last breath in front of him; because of him. All I needed to do was be nicer and not cause trouble. I loved him a lot and I was sure that if I did more he would stop getting angry.

"No Paul, I don't remember. It was just a dream."

"Are you sure you're not seeing anybody else?"

"No Paul, I'm not seeing anyone. Where on earth would I in any case meet anybody or have the time to see anybody? I don't have friends and I don't see anyone at work except for Ronell and Susan. So where on earth do you think I would find the time to have another relationship? You drop me off at work and pick me up. I don't even go to the shops by myself and when was the last time I met my sister on my own, I can't even recall? So no, I don't have someone else and I don't know or have control over what I was dreaming about, ok?"

He just stared at me, turned on his heel and walked away. I wished he had closed the door behind him, but I would be so lucky to have privacy in my own flat. I couldn't even remember when last I was alone. If I was at work, I had Ronell and Susan around me. I got picked up from work by Paul and if he couldn't be around me for some reason after work, I would get dropped off at his Mom's house where either Mandy, Amy, the two kids, the maid or his Mom would keep me company till he got back. Only then was I allowed to go back to the flat, where he now slept every night. Is this how life in a relationship is supposed to be? No breathing space at all?

The only time I was alone and in my happy place, was early in the morning when I would wake up before opening my eyes. I needed more of that alone time, time in my mind, in my happy place, where my imagination could take me wherever I wanted to go.

I just couldn't wake up with a smile again, not ever again.

Another thing that started happening soon after we moved to Francesca, Paul started to play a little game with me. At least, that's what he called it. He would pin me down on the floor and flick his lighter in my face. Sometimes so close that I would close my eyes because I was so scared the flame was going to burn me. He would laugh and say, "Azelene, the sooner you open your eyes the sooner I'll move the lighter further away. Shut your eyes and I'll keep coming closer." He would then smirk and say, "This is how you build trust my darling." For me it had nothing to do with trust, it was frightening and sadistic. But I was too scared to argue, so I did what he said and forced my eyes open. To this day I have a fear of things close to my face and sudden movements in front of my eyes. I have flashbacks, which are very upsetting because they remind me of him and what he took from me.

Chapter 15

Punching bag by day, Hustler by night!

We didn't go out often, but Paul loved playing pool. Playing pool on weekends was our escape. He taught me to play and I did well on the tables, hustling and winning big money. I played for about three months with him, when he decided to buy me a new cue. I was so pleased and loved my cue and lived for evenings out on the town proving myself at the tables. We won most nights and never had any issues when we played. Paul never drank anything while we played; the best times were when he didn't drink anything. I used to sip on a Bacardi Breezer, but never drank more than one.

One evening we played a couple of new guys and won. Then Paul decided to play a round of singles with one of them. His partner came up to me and asked if I wanted something to drink. My Breezer was finished, so I accepted his offer. He bought me a drink and we stood on the sideline cheering our partners on, chatting in between and laughing and joking. Paul finished the game with no effort. It was very strange that he challenged the guy in the first place, because he didn't play well at all. In fact, his friend who was standing on the sidelines with me was a far better player. What was Paul thinking? He walked over to me and grabbed my arm.

"Are you done?" I stared at him, shocked.
"What do you mean?" I asked, confused.
"Are you done making a fool out of me?"
"Paul, I don't understand what you mean!"
"You're acting as if you're available, Azelene. Get your bag, we're leaving." I grabbed my bag, picked up my pool cue and walked out the door after him. He spun round and grabbed the pool cue out of my hand.

"You won't need this anymore!" He took it in both hands, lifted his knee and broke my cue in two, threw it on the floor and walked away. I stood there with tears in my eyes looking at him, wondering what the hell was going on in his head. Why was he doing things to create issues that made me look like the troublemaker? I didn't understand his motives, his reasons and what he was gaining from it all. We got in the car and neither of us spoke the whole way back to my flat. I took a bath and got into bed. I sobbed myself to sleep. I was so depressed; I was alone, and I felt defeated.

I was never allowed to play again. Paul still played on Friday and Saturday nights, but after that fateful evening, I was never allowed close to the table. One evening, one of the regulars was chatting to Paul.

"What's wrong? Why isn't Azelene playing tonight?" he asked.

"She doesn't like playing anymore; she gave her cue away a couple of weeks ago. Now she just tags along to watch me," Paul said as he looked at me.

I sat there and thought to myself, "If you only knew how badly I want to play", but I wasn't allowed to touch a cue ever again. It broke my heart to sit there every weekend, knowing I wasn't allowed to join in anymore.

Things were being taken away from me bit by bit, my personality, my dignity, my pride, my love for life. I felt alone, sad, unwanted and guilty. But I never told anyone about what was going on behind closed doors. I wore a mask, a mask that hid so much pain. We didn't have friends, I didn't see my family anymore, Ronell and I only talked at work and I wasn't allowed to visit her anymore. It was now just Paul, his family and I, and he checked my every move. I never even went home to visit my parents; we only spoke on the phone once in a while. I felt isolated but didn't know how to turn things around. I was very young and not nearly mature enough to know what to do or who to talk to and that made everything so much worse.

Chapter 16

The Dress

"Great spirits have always encountered violent opposition from mediocre minds."
-Albert Einstein-

One Friday afternoon we got ready to go to a modeling show that Mandy was taking part in in Johannesburg. Paul told me that Jack and his girlfriend were in town and that they would be joining us that evening. I liked him a lot and couldn't wait to meet his new lady. Paul ran me a bath and said he would get my clothes out. I followed his instructions and climbed in the tub. After my bath, he told me to sit so that he could dry my hair. My dress was already on the bed with shoes, my bag and earrings. I went and sat in front of the mirror and looked over my shoulder at the dress on the bed and thought to myself, "I'm so glad he took the short polka dot out." I loved it and felt fantastic in it. I hadn't worn it much because we didn't go places where it was appropriate, but a modeling show was perfect. In a way, I was a bit sad that I would not be on stage myself that evening. Paul didn't want me to further my modeling career, so I flicked the thought out of my mind and looked at myself in the mirror again. Paul stood behind me and started combing my hair.

Suddenly the movie Sleeping with the Enemy popped into my head and I got a cold shiver down my spine. Is this what normal couples do? Do their partners decide what they wear, do their hair and take all their freedom away? I knew this wasn't right but what were my options? Shortly after Paul finished my hair and I got dressed, the doorbell rang. Jack and his girlfriend were on time. He arrived with a cold bottle of champagne and we decided to have a glass before we left for the show. I was very excited and looking forward to a night out on the town.

We arrived in Johannesburg and enjoyed an evening of glitz and glamour. I felt like a million dollars and was able to see myself on stage with all the other girls. I missed my modeling. Suddenly I missed Peter as well. I couldn't get him out of my mind for most of the evening. After the show, Paul and Jack suggested that we go out for dinner. We were all hungry and Jack said he knew of a great place in Sandton. Excitedly, we jumped in the car. Paul was driving, and Jack and his girlfriend sat in the back. We chatted happily, and the evening felt perfect. I hadn't had a perfect day or night in such a long time, so I was excited and enjoying every minute of it. We parked the car and got out. Paul and I walked hand in hand towards the restaurant. As we approached the entrance, a handsome guy and his beautiful girlfriend came walking towards us, as they made their way to their car.

"Wow, she looks beautiful," the man said to his partner.

"Yes, I love her dress," she replied, looking at me. I smiled and felt so good about myself, but suddenly Paul stopped, took his jacket off and pointed at me.

"Put my jacket on," he hissed.

"Thanks, but I'm not cold, I don't need your jacket," I responded.

"I'm not asking you Azelene; I'm telling you to put my jacket on now!" Paul barked at me. Jack and his girlfriend just kept on walking.

He draped his jacket over my shoulders. "Let's go."

Suddenly the warm, happy atmosphere had changed. We walked into the restaurant and when I got to the table, I lifted my hand towards my shoulder to take the jacket off and place it over the chair.

"Don't you dare," Paul ground out, putting his hand on my back in warning. I sat down and had the most uncomfortable dinner ever.

When I stood up to go to the toilet, Paul walked with me. I thought to myself, "Thank God he isn't allowed in the Ladies, because I know he would follow me in just to make sure I wasn't alone." I closed the cubicle door behind me, pulled the jacket off and threw it on the floor. I thought furiously, "You are a fucking bastard!" When I was done, I went and stood in front of the mirror, looking at the skinny girl staring back at me. I was still pretty, but I was so extremely sad and wanted to cry. I took the jacket and draped it over my shoulders once again. Seeing myself disappearing under this enormous jacket broke my heart. I was scared, and I didn't know where to turn.

Doing as I was told was always the best option when things turned sour, because if I tried to stand up for myself I knew I might end up with another black eye. I walked out and saw the look of irritation on his face. "Why'd you take so long?" I didn't answer, just continued walking to the table where Jack and his new girlfriend were sitting obliviously chatting and laughing.

After dinner, we got back in the car to go home. Paul asked Jack if he would drive and offered up a lame excuse for why he couldn't.

"Anytime," Jack said, and Paul and I got in the back seat. It was dark and quiet. Paul asked Jack to turn the music up and as soon as it was loud enough, I felt the blows rain down on my thighs. He hit me hard, over and over again. I bent forward and begged him to stop but he grabbed me by the back of the head and head-butted me with such force that I knew it was going to result in another black eye. I reeled back and saw Jack looking at me in the rearview mirror. Paul continued his assault on my thighs and I curled my head to my knees in a desperate attempt to protect myself. When we got to the flat, Paul climbed out and went inside without so much as a backward glance. I stayed in the car, crying.

"Why didn't you do something?" I asked Jack as they climbed out of the vehicle, but he just looked at me.

"What do you mean Azelene?"

"You must have seen what happened, Jack? Paul just head butted me in the car. Look at my eye."

"Sorry Azelene, but I didn't see anything." He took his girlfriend's hand and they walked away, leaving me standing alone outside my flat. I had a pounding headache and was terrified to go inside. When I finally screwed up the courage, I found Paul fast asleep in bed. Again, I was shocked to see how easily he was able to fall asleep after such an outburst of rage and hatred. I walked into the bathroom, shut and locked the door. I sat down on the closed toilet seat and pulled my dress up. My legs were blue, they were sore and bruised. I placed my face in my hands and started to sob like a baby. I wanted to go home, I wanted to be protected, I wanted to be far away from this man, but I was scared and didn't know how to get out of the situation I was in. I stayed in the bathroom for a long time crying and feeling extremely sorry for myself.

The next morning Paul didn't say a word. It was all forgotten. Everything seemed normal again. He woke up early and went down to the local bakery to get us freshly baked croissants. I decided to stay in bed; my eye was blue and swollen and I felt bruised and sore. Paul came back and walked into the room with an enormous bunch of fresh flowers and dropped them next to me on the bed.

"Here you go," he said. "Hope this will cheer you up." I just looked at him silently.

The rest of the week passed without any issues.

*"His worst fantasy, her reality,
He pulls the strings
Does unspeakable things
A sadistic entrance for his acceptance."*

-Diana Rasmussen-

Chapter 17

Mickey

"You can judge a man's true character, by the way, he treats his fellow animals,"
~Paul McCartney~

From that point on, things started to go downhill fast. I realised that Paul didn't have to look for a reason to abuse me; he would create situations and blame it on me. Then blame me for his actions. I got used to the emotional abuse on a daily basis, but the physical attacks seemed to happen on a cyclical basis. There would be a couple of weeks buildup between outbursts. Back then I didn't realise it was a pattern. I was afraid of him; I was scared that he would once again try to kill me, like the day he pulled the trigger and missed me by centimeters. The problem was, I didn't know when that day would finally arrive. Things were already building up to the next outburst, which could have been about anything.

One Saturday Paul and I drove to a nursery not far from where we lived, to buy a plant for the flat. There was a litter of kittens walking around the premises. One of them was so adorable; I picked him up and carried him around while we looked for the perfect plant. When we got to the till, I asked the lady if the kittens were for sale. She explained that they would give them away for free to a good home. I thought to myself, "I would love one, but I don't have a safe home for him to grow up in." Our home was toxic, with way too much pain and sadness in the air. She asked me if I wanted one and I told her that if I could get one, I would have taken this one. I loved him already. She smiled and rang the plant up. After we paid, and I started to walk away, she called after me.

"Miss, if you change your mind, I'm taking them to the SPCA early next week." I just smiled sadly, knowing that I would have loved one.

The New Year was approaching, and I wondered what lay ahead for me. I was quite enjoying my new job and loved my flat, but there was something missing.

A few days later, Paul picked me up at work and said that his mother had invited us to dinner and asked if I wanted to stop at the flat before we went to the house. I told him no, that I didn't need to anything at the apartment, so we drove straight over. When we arrived, Paul told me to wait outside. He went in and left me standing in front of the house. Seconds later he came back with his hands held out and a towel thrown over them. He said to me, "Azelene can you lift the towel?" I took one corner of the towel and pulled it off. In his hands was the kitten that I had cuddled at the nursery a couple of days earlier.

"You have no idea how long it took me to locate this little guy! When I got back to the nursery, they told me that the owner had taken them away two days ago. They couldn't find the owner and I remembered that she had said she was going to take them to the SPCA. But, when I arrived they told me they weren't there. They sent me to three pet shops and eventually I located him at the last pet store I went to." I took him out of Paul's hands and started to cry. He was the most beautiful cat I had ever seen.

"Thank you so much, Paul. I wanted this kitten so badly."

"I'm glad you're happy with him. I hope that he will bring you lots of love and happiness in the years to come," Paul said, smiling at us.

"I am going to call him Mickey."

Chapter 18

You can call me anytime!

The evening started badly. When we arrived home, Paul was in a foul mood, it was one of those evenings where he went out of his way to belittle me. From the minute we walked in the door the emotional abuse began. He started asking me the same old questions, questions I wasn't able to answer because no matter which way I replied, he would find a reason why my answer was wrong. I decided to start doing the laundry to try and avoid him but walking away was never a good idea. As soon as I turned my back on him, he grabbed me by the arm and slapped me across the face.

"You will not walk away from me when I'm talking to you Azelene. What the fuck is wrong with you?" He growled.

"Paul you're hurting me, please leave my arm." I begged. Paul just tightened his grip further, until I started crying. My arm was going numb and my cheek was burning. I didn't dare touch it, because I knew he would slap me again. He started shaking me then pushed me away from him shouting,

"Get out of my face! Go do the washing, that's all you're good for anyway!" I fell from the impact of his push and knocked my head against the cupboard. I pulled myself up and walked to the bathroom where my washing machine stood and started on the laundry. I wished that I was able to close the door and hide from this monster. But there was no hiding from him. So much dark hatred seeped into my heart. I wanted to run away but where could I go, there was no support for me because nobody knew what was going on. I was alone in this.

The next morning, I went to work and had my excuses all lined up for the marks on my face and upper arm. I didn't talk too much and tried to hide my feelings from Ronell and Susan. I didn't want them to know what was going on. I went out for regular smoke breaks and felt like crying every time I stood on the cold stairs smoking and thinking about the home I was going back to that evening. I was scared to go back, but I didn't have any other option.

That afternoon when I left work, Ronell called me back just before I walked out the office. She looked me straight in the eyes.

"Azelene, I just wanted you to know that you can phone me any time of the day or night if you need me. I don't care what it is or where you are. If you need somebody, I'm there for you, anytime!" I looked at her and said thanks, turned around and walked out the office. I burst into tears as soon as I closed the door, knowing in my heart, that Ronell knew more than she let on. She knew Paul was beating me on a regular basis. I saw it in her eyes, even though she didn't say it in so many words. I walked home that afternoon. Paul told me he had clients with him at the flat, looking over plans, and that he wouldn't be able to pick me up after work. I looked forward to walking home even though it was only two blocks. That was enough alone time for me, to collect myself and dry my eyes before I walked into the flat.

Chapter 19

Do I look like a dog?

By the time I arrived my tears were dry, my smile was back, and I walked in with a friendly face to show Paul's clients what an amazing, loving couple we were. I introduced myself to them, greeted Paul with a warm hug and a kiss and asked if anyone wanted coffee. I left the living room and walked back in 5 minutes later with four steaming mugs. The couple was very friendly, and I went and sat down with them at the table, listening to them going through their home plans, new ideas and the changes they wanted to make. They left just after 11 pm, happy with the revisions and on a mission to get the house plans approved. After they left, I asked Paul if he was hungry as we hadn't eaten yet. He said yes and went and lay on the bed. I went to the kitchen and started making fish and chips. It was late; I was tired and wanted to make something quick and easy, so we could get to bed. When the food was ready, I walked into the room and handed him his plate. Paul pushed himself up on his elbow and looked down at it.

With one flick, he slapped the food out of my hands into the air. Fish and chips rained down on top of me. He jumped up and grabbed me by the throat.

"Do I look like a dog to you? Not even my dog would eat this shit." He dragged me into the living room and threw me against the wall. Grabbing me by my hair, he pulled me to the middle of the floor and started kicking me in the stomach. He snatched up a cushion, placed it over my face and started punching me through the cushion with his fist, to dampen the sound and to cover my mouth so I couldn't scream.

It's close to midnight, on a Saturday evening in early January 1993, but instead of revelling in the party atmosphere of the New Year like most 20-year-olds, I am lying completely motionless on the cold, hard floor of my living room.

I can faintly hear the late-night traffic outside the open window of my second-floor apartment facing Pretorius Street in Pretoria, South Africa. Fighting the blackness that threatens to consume me, I try to entertain the thought of calling for help. I know it is pointless.

I lick my lips and recognise the familiar metallic tang of my blood in my mouth. The dark blue carpet in my living room feels like sandpaper under my bruised and battered face. I close my eyes and let a single tear slip down my cheek, leaving a trail of memories and broken promises in its wake.

Lying broken in a fetal position with one eye still closed. My thoughts turn to my mother. Strangely, I wonder what she might be doing. I think about what she would do if she knew what was happening to her daughter right this moment. Would she pick me up and hold me and pacify me like she did when I was little?

Would she be disappointed that I didn't recognise the warning signs and ask for help?

Deep down in my heart, I know that she would gently stroke my hair and smile sweetly at me and tell me it was going to be ok - I was going to be ok. With that thought in my mind, a smile flickers across my face, and I feel momentarily at peace.

This mirage of safety is ripped apart when I feel the sharp metal spurs of his boots penetrate the skin on my back. And I scream, a deep primal continuous scream as he kicks me over and over again - without mercy and remorse. What have I done to deserve this? How am I going to escape the pure rage and hatred of this man?

My final thought before losing consciousness is the panicked realization that this is the night I am going to die. He is finally going to kill me, and it will be a long, slow, lonely and very painful death. I'm not sure how long I was out. What I do remember was hearing the beat of my heart and realising I was still alive. At that point, I wasn't convinced I actually wanted to be alive. I lay there with my eyes closed, too scared to open them. I wasn't sure where he was. I was still able to hear the traffic outside the window, but inside the flat was quiet. I felt another warm tear rolling down my face. I opened my good eye a little, where I was still lying on the carpet in a fetal position and gazed straight at him as he lay passed out on my couch, my flat's key hanging halfway out his pocket. I heard a faint snore and knew he was asleep. I tried to get up, but my body was broken, battered and I was wracked with pain from head to toe. I fell back, exhausted and started crying softly.

But then a sliver of hope changed my mind and I knew I had to get out. I opened my eyes again and started pulling myself across the carpet on my side, telling myself to move slowly until I was closer to the couch. I lifted my hand and touched the pink key holder that was hanging out of his pocket. I took it between my thumb and forefinger and pulled, but it was stuck. I pulled gently again and again. Suddenly Paul turned onto his side and the key fell out of his pocket straight into my hand. I closed my fist and dropped my head on my arms, pretending to be asleep, just in case I had woken him. I lay there for five long minutes. It felt like an hour. I had to make sure he was still sleeping. Finally, I was able to crawl over to the far side of the living room where I grabbed Mickey, who was sitting in the corner, scared and bewildered. I threw him into my blood soaked, ripped nightgown.

There was no time to get dressed; I needed to escape as quickly and quietly as possible. I jumped up and ran to the front door, unlocked it and ran down the stairs. I didn't know if Paul would wake up, but I was sure as hell not going to wait around to find out! I stumbled to where my red 50cc scooter was in the undercover parking. Climbing on with Mickey safely tucked away inside the front of my nightgown, I gathered the rest of it under my bum and between my legs, so he wouldn't fall out while I was riding. I started my bike and drove down Pretorius Street, which was a one-way road, heading west. On impulse I decided to turn and drive in the wrong direction in case Paul was behind me, that way he would not be able to follow me driving in a car against the flow of traffic. This would buy me some time to get away. I was totally in charge and knew what I had to do. I arrived at Sunnyside Police Station, parked my bike and ran inside. I was in a lot of pain and looked like I had just emerged from a war zone. I shouted at the police officer behind the counter.

"Please help me! My boyfriend beat me up and he's still in my flat. I want to make a case against him."

"Now what have you done to deserve this? You must have done something?" the officer asked, looking me up and down.

"Fuck you!" was all I was able to think of at that point, to express my shock and desperation. I turned and ran out of the station. When I got to the sidewalk, a young constable caught up with me.

"Stop, stop, come back. My mom will help you; my mom has experienced this herself. She works here on day shift. I'll call her to take your statement. Please come back, I'll help you."

I started sobbing like a small, frightened child, knowing that if I didn't go back inside with him I would have to return home and that was the last place I wanted to be. He took my hand gently.

"Don't be scared, I won't hurt you." He took me into a small office and came back a couple of minutes later with sugar water and told me that his mother was on her way.

"My Mom used to give me sugar water. Thank you." I quavered, weakly. He smiled. I asked if there was a place I could wash up.

"Not now," he replied, explaining that his Mom had to see me first. "She might need to take some photos too." I took Mickey out from under my nightgown and placed him on my lap. He was uncharacteristically still, and I could see the fear in his eyes. Mickey hadn't liked Paul from the beginning. Soon after I got him, he started to pee on Paul's side of the bed. Wherever Paul's clothes were lying he would pee on them and once he peed on Paul's lap. So, I think he was only too happy to be out of the flat. I knew that Paul would have killed Mickey if he had woken up and found I wasn't there. He was going to go nuts when he realised I was gone. I had just finished my sugar water when a tall blond woman walked in. Even though she tried her best to keep a poker face when she saw me, I could tell she was saddened by what she saw.

"You poor girl, do you need anything?" She enquired gently. I shook my head and looked down at Mickey, now fast asleep on my lap.

"Azelene, I'm Captain Lauren McKenzie. I'll be taking your statement tonight. Is there anything I can get you?" She asked me a second time.

"No thank you, I don't need anything. I just want to clean up." I replied.

"I know it's very hard for you, but we need all the evidence we can get if you're going to make a case against the person who did this to you. I'll try my best to get through everything as quickly as possible. But from here I'll need to send you over to the hospital for an internal and external examination. Do you want to phone anyone?"

"Not now, I want to talk to you first; I'm not sure what to do. My family doesn't know about my abusive relationship."

"I need to ask you a couple of questions, would that be ok?" I nodded mutely.

"Please state your full name for me?"

"Azelene Riekert"

"How old are you?"

"19, I am turning 20 next week."

"Where do you live and with whom?"

"Francesca Flats, Pretorius Street,"

The questions continued, and I answered them with a distant voice. I was angry, I was suddenly furious. Why was I now forced to sit in a small, cold office in a police station? Answering questions that I didn't want to answer, while Paul was still in my flat sleeping, oblivious to what was happening on the other side of town? Or did he know? Had he woken up at some point? Was he looking for me? I could just imagine how angry he would be if he knew where I was. But I'd had enough.

I didn't want to be a punching bag anymore. I didn't want to cry myself to sleep anymore. I didn't want to cover up my bruises anymore. I didn't want to lie to my family anymore or fear death or feel isolated. I didn't want to be sworn at anymore. I didn't want to wear the mask anymore, a mask that covered my pain, my sadness, my fear, my disappointment, my hate, my anger towards this man.

I was broken, and I wanted to break the silence, I wanted to stand on a hill and shout it out for the entire world to hear. But I was still sitting in this cold office being bombarded with questions that hurt so much. Again, my thoughts turned to my mother and I wondered how this would make her feel, seeing me sitting here so pitiful, disheveled and sad. I was sure it would kill her. I decided it was better she wasn't here. I had to deal with this on my own for now. Lauren finished the interview off and told me she was going to send two constables to my flat to throw Paul out. They would lock up and bring the key back to the police station. Lauren asked who I wanted to phone, and I said that I wanted to call my sister. It was late when I heard Ronell's home phone ringing in my ear. When she answered, all I was able to muster was, "I'm at Sunnyside Police Station, can you please come and get me?"

"I'm on my way," was all she said before slamming the phone down. It didn't bother me, because I suspected she had been waiting for this call. A half hour later Ronell walked into the police station with her arms open.

"My poor sister, are you ok? Look what he's done to you! I'll kill that man with my bare hands. Azelene, I'm so glad you called me!" I looked at her without any emotion; I felt like a freak, as though I had no tear ducts. In my heart, I wanted to cry and cry and cry. But at the same time, I was hard as a rock with anger buried deep inside me.

"You need to take me to the State Hospital to be examined. I need to get a report from them if I'm going to make a case against him." She took my hand.
"Come, Stefan is in the car – we'll go home to drop him off and we may as well leave the cat at home too and then we can go to the hospital." We walked out of the station and I told Lauren that I would pick my bike up the next day. They moved it to the back where it would

be safe. As we were leaving, the two officers arrived back from my flat and handed me the keys. I asked them what had happened, and they advised me that when they arrived my front door was still open as I had left it and Paul was still fast asleep. When they woke him up he got the fright of his life, seeing them standing there. They told him that I was going to make a case against him and that I would be getting a restraining order too. They instructed him to leave my flat and that he was not allowed to take anything with him except his car keys. I was relieved that he was gone, but still scared that he would make his way back. I wished that they had handcuffed him, locked him up and thrown away the key. Knowing his luck, he would have a warm bed at his mother's house to sleep in.

     I thanked them and got into the car. We drove in silence to Ronell and Stefan's house. Ronell didn't ask me any questions and I wasn't in a chatty mood. When we got there, she took Mickey inside. Then we drove to Hospital and I walked over to the reception with my letter from Lauren. The lady took all my details down, showed me to a bed and asked me to wait there. The bed was in a large ward with lots of other beds filled with moaning patients and crying babies. I sat waiting for a long time.

     Eventually, a doctor arrived and started my examination. It was the most humiliating thing I had ever experienced. I had to take all my clothes off and every single mark on my body was measured, photographed and annotated. Only when I took my nightgown off, did I see the big bruise on my rib cage where Paul had kicked me over and over again. There was also a large mark on my abdomen. I was struggling to breathe, and the doctor said he would need to send me for x-rays after the examination was over. He then did an internal exam and that made me feel even more vulnerable and upset. They wanted to make sure that I hadn't been raped, even though I told him I hadn't had intercourse with Paul in over a week. The doctor asked me to pull my legs up and open them. I felt the cold speculum slip into my vagina and cried for the first time. I was cold, alone and in extreme pain. I felt violated and hated Paul more and more, but I knew that I had reached the point of no return. I knew that I would never go back to him again.

For more than three years Paul had treated me like his slave, he had used and abused me. At this point I wasn't sure which scars were worse, the physical ones or the emotional ones. But it was far from over. The most difficult part was going to be facing my parents and telling them what had happened. Where did I start? How did I begin explaining why I never told them? Why I kept quiet, why I didn't trust them enough to share my nightmare with them. What I did know was that I wasn't ready to talk just yet. I wanted to get out of this hospital and sink into a warm, comforting bath. I wanted to scrub the marks of pain away. I wanted to soak in the water till I was clean, and all the blood was washed away. Even then, I wanted to stay in the bath longer, hoping that the pain inside my heart would be washed away too. But that was wishful thinking. All I got from staying too long in the tub were wrinkled fingertips. I wanted it all to be just a story and not part of my life. But I was the main character in this horrible, psychotic tale.

As soon as the doctor had completed his internal examination, he instructed me to go over to the radiology department as he wanted a chest x-ray. The x-ray confirmed that I had fractured ribs. Now I knew why I found it so difficult to breathe. The doctor strapped me up and said that it would help me to breathe a little easier. As a child, I once ran into our kitchen counter at home, when I slipped on oil on the floor, banged my ribcage into the corner of the counter and cracked a rib. So, I knew what the procedure was for a cracked or fractured rib. Shortly after he completed his examination, the doctor gave me a prescription for strong painkillers and sent me home.

We walked out of the hospital at around 6:30 in the morning. The sun was shining, and the birds were singing. It was a new day and I wasn't looking forward to it. I wanted to climb into bed, hide my head under the blankets and stay there. I didn't want to face this day.

We drove back to Ronell's home.

"Az, I'm here if you want to talk. I'm not going to push you to tell me what happened, and I'll tell Mom and Dad the same thing. I promise we won't bombard you with questions. When you're ready, we'll be here. If you don't want to talk that's also ok. When you went in for the x-ray, the doctor gave me a letter, referring you to a psychiatrist. Maybe it would be good for you to talk to her, but only when you're ready." Ronell promised.

"I'll go see her." I replied, "I need to speak to someone outside our family circle about what's happened. I won't be able to get through this without help."

"Ok, then we'll make an appointment for you soon."

When we got home, Ronell went and made a nice warm bubble bath for me. I was able to take the bandage off when I bathed and showered, and Ronell was able to help me put it back on again.

It felt good, but my skin was stinging all over and my body was in pain. Ronell said that she would phone Mom and Dad and tell them what had happened. When I got out of the bath, she gave me a glass of milk to drink with sugar and vanilla in.

"Drink this and go climb into bed when you're finished Azelene. Your pills are on the bedside table, take them and get some sleep. Sleep as long as you want to." The pills knocked me out. I slept for a few hours and woke up in the late afternoon. I was hungry, and my body was now in even more pain. The mark from where Paul had grabbed me around the neck was also now more visible and the ones where he kicked me in the chest and abdomen were bigger and bluer. It looked painful and it was. I told Ronell I needed some clean clothes and she promised to take me to my flat the following morning to get some of my things.

The next day at around 9:00 o'clock we drove to my flat, so I could pack a bag. I had decided to stay at Ronell's house for a couple of days. It was safer than my flat at this point. I wasn't sure what Paul's plans were for me, but I was scared of him and knew that I didn't have the strength to face him right now.

When we arrived, I paused at the door for a couple of seconds. Ronell turned to me and said "Az, don't worry he isn't here, the police gave you his key. It's ok to go in. I'm here with you." I unlocked the door and walked in. I was still able to smell his aftershave inside. It nauseated me. Suddenly I felt sick to my stomach and I ran to the bathroom, collapsed in front of the toilet on my knees and started vomiting. I think it was a combination of pain and revulsion that made me so sick. The next moment I heard Ronell's voice.

"Hello Mandy," I picked my head up from the toilet bowl and dragged myself to my feet. I wiped my mouth with the back of my hand and walked out of the bathroom. There I saw Mandy and her mother at my front door.

"Hello Ronell, Hello Azelene, may we come in?" Mandy walked towards me arms, outstretched to give me a hug. I lifted my left hand up between us and stopped her in her tracks.

"Don't come close to me, don't touch me Mandy." She backed off, walked over to the couch and sat down. Paul's Mom had a small plant in one hand and a bunch of flowers in the other. She held the flowers out to me and said, "These are from Mandy and I, the little love palm is from Paul." I started to laugh.

"Very, very fucking inappropriate. Thank you but you can take that back, in fact, you can take the flowers back too. What do you want?" I asked her incredulously.

"Azelene, Paul told us what happened, and he feels so bad, he wanted us to come and see how you were doing?" I lift the t-shirt that I had borrowed from

Ronell up and said, "This is what I look like, and what I feel like well, that is very difficult to explain. I'm bruised, torn apart, sore, scared, confused, disappointed. Do you understand?"

Paul's Mom dropped her head and said softly, "It doesn't look that bad. The bruises will heal quickly, don't worry."

"You must be kidding me! Are you for real? Did I hear you right? The bruises will heal quickly! What about the scars inside? Mandy, please tell me that your Mom is kidding! Is that all she's able to say to me? You know what, I think you should leave. I have nothing to say to you, your Mom or your brother." I almost shouted. They stood up, Paul's Mom still holding onto the love palm and flowers and left my flat without another word. I shook my head in disbelief.

"Did you see any sympathy or empathy? Their eyes were dead!" I spluttered at Ronell. I walked over to the cupboard and started packing my things. I wasn't sure how long my stay with Ronell would be, but I knew I wasn't ready to stay in this flat right now. My Mom decided to hunt Desi, Paul's x-girlfriend down. Desi told my mom that Paul use to beat her up on a daily basis. That's why she left him. Also, that she wanted to warn me years ago when she walked into the bathroom at the restaurant but was scared that I would think it was sour grapes, so she left it.

Chapter 20

Too close for Comfort

I stayed with Ronell for a couple of days and took off work while I was there. By the time I decided I was able to move back to my flat, I had a restraining order in place. Paul was not allowed to come within 200m of me. I wasn't sure if the restraining order would keep me safe; but it gave me peace of mind, that if he did try something he would be arrested and locked up. I didn't see Paul again after that fateful day, until many years later. At that point, I was still married to my ex-husband Johan Smalberger. Paul was doing some renovations on the house opposite the one we were renting. I wasn't aware of that. I knew there were men working there and I saw someone sitting in a pickup truck in the mornings when I left for work, but I never saw his face.

One afternoon I got a call from the estate agent we had rented our house from. She asked me if she could bring a contractor to the house, to get a quote on some work the owner wanted done. I agreed and made arrangements to meet her at the house after work.

There was a knock on the door and when I opened it, there was the agent with Paul standing next to her. I got such a fright I slammed the door shut.

When I opened it again, I apologised and asked them to come in. "No problem Azelene, this is Paul. Paul this is......" "Azelene, yes I know her very well. Hello, Azelene." Paul said. I heard my name fall out of his mouth. The first thing I realised was that he hadn't changed at all. He was still very handsome and for a moment I stared into his eyes trying to see what he was thinking. "Come in Suzanne, please hurry, I need to leave in about 5 minutes." I heard myself lying to her. This poor woman didn't have a clue about what had happened between us; she didn't know who this monster was. She took him to the back of the house and showed him the work that needed doing. They left without Paul saying another word to me.

After they had gone, I called Suzanne and asked her to please never bring him to the house again, explaining that I had a restraining order against him. She felt really bad and promised me she would pass the message on to the owner as well. I walked into the living room after our conversation and stood with my back against the cold wall. I started to cry and suddenly all the emotions came flooding back. I'm not sure how long I cried, but I did feel better when it was over. What I then realised was, I wasn't scared of him anymore. In fact, I was hoping to see him again, so I could tell him so, but after that day I have never had the opportunity to do so.

Once more I was reminded that I was exceptionally lucky to have escaped with my life.
Unfortunately, although no longer afraid of the man, he had stolen my innocence and abused my love and trust

in him, and worst of all taught me how to hate for the first time in my life. It took me years to trust again. What I thought was love was abuse. When I gave consent, I was actually sexually abused.

Chapter 21

Present Day 2021

Author | Domestic Violence Advocate | Program Facilitator | Motivational Speaker | Youth Mentor Holistic Counsellor | Social Worker

In addition to being a wife and mother, Azelene is a highly passionate, people-centred professional, who has acquired over nine years' experience delivering community programs and services. Inspired by her own personal traumatic experiences, she is determined to pursue social justice whilst supporting individuals to build their confidence, capabilities, and skillset in achieving desired outcomes from their own fear to freedom. Azelene is an internationally published author, a registered Holistic Counsellor, and has completed a Bachelor of Social Work at Edith Cowan University in 2020. She uses her lived experience and theory related to Family and Domestic Violence to educate others. She shook the hands of many politicians including Australia's current Prime Minister Scott Morrison and the former Prime Minister Malcolm

Turnbull. In 2018 she was a guest at the Loge in Canberra which is the primary official residence of the Prime Minister of Australia. She has visited the Parliament house in Perth and in Canberra as a guest of Senator the Hon Michaelia Cash Minister for Employment, Skills, Small and Family Business with her husband and daughter Sian Williams the founder of Kidzucate. She was interviewed on Channel 7, Channel 9, Channel 10, SBS and ABC TV, and most of the well-known radio stations and newspapers nationally and internationally, as CEO and Co-founder of Kidzucate. She has spoken and delivered programs in schools, universities, organisations and corporate companies. Azelene have also spoken at events locally and internationally. She has set up a charity from scratch and organised amazing fundraisers over the years. She is highly regarded both on and offline, and her friends and followers mention that she is inspiring and empowers men, women and children all over the world. They say; "Azelene is a kind-hearted, pro-active and honest person, who is creating opportunities where people she advocates for see no hope". She has published four books and has received numerous awards and nominations over the years. Her passion is to educate teens and adults about healthy relationships, how to identify an abusive relationship, help them to put strategies in place to break free and to provide them with information on appropriate support services. She has proven success in developing strong, trusted relationships with individuals from diverse age groups, organisational levels, cultural heritages, and socio-economic backgrounds by combining exceptional communication, interpersonal and mediation skills with industry-leading therapeutic methodologies. As a social activist, Azelene is determined to make a positive impact on individuals and in communities. Originally from South Africa, she lived in the Middle East before settling in Perth, Western Australia in 2011 with her husband and only daughter. She experienced three and a half years of physical and emotional abuse as a teenager in her first relationship and came out a stronger person who life ambition as an activist in the field of domestic and family violence is to have a positive impact both on today's and future generations. Azelene is currently aligned with the following organisations WA Child Safety Services where she delivers healthy relationship programs in schools, Ruah communities as a media advocate, Anglicare as a community educator and Patricia Giles as a kids and teen counsellor. Azelene also has a small holistic counselling private practice called From Fear to Freedom and would never shy away from any opportunity to collaborate with other organisations to make a difference. In her off time, she's a keen deep-sea fisher who took part in three Marlin Classics over the years. And loves spending time with her husband and her daughter Sian. Her dad passed away in 1999, and her mother and sister still live in South Africa. She is happily married to her husband Glyn Williams and enjoys life with him and her only daughter in Perth, Australia. A place she calls home.

To Book Azelene as Domestic Violence Keynote Speaker or to find out more about the programs she delivers in schools contact her directly via:
www.azelenewilliams.com or azelenewilliams@gmail.com

Azelene is an engaging presenter. Throughout Azelene's sessions, she draws on her personal experience as a survivor of intimate partner violence as a teenager. In her lived experience presentation, she talks about key concepts, theory and different forms of abuse and connects them to her lived experience. She explains the cycle of abuse in-depth and presents her speech to the audience with a passion you can feel in the room. All presentations conclude with open question time, where the audience has the opportunity and is encouraged to ask questions that will further help them understand what intimate partner violence, consent and coercion look like in real life.

Some of the schools Azelene delivered programs to includes but is not limited to the following:

- Helena College
- La Salle College
- Lake Joondalup Baptist College
- Penrhos College
- Santa Maria College
- St Mark's Anglican Community School
- Swan Valley ACS
- John Septimus Roe
- John Wollaston ACS

Azelene vowed not to let her dyslexia stop her from developing new skills. She has done phenomenally well over the years to educate herself.

Educational Background
- Bachelor of Social Work *Institution: ECU – 2020*
- Diploma in CBT: Centre of Excellence - 2021
- Dip. Community Services Work *Institution: TYFE* – 2014
- Cert. Sexual Intelligence Professional Training *Institution: Relationships Australia* – 2013
- Dip. Holistic Counselling – Sand tray, Clay and Art Therapy *Institution: Sophia College* – 2012

Professional Development and Training
- Safe & Together Model CORE Training – Safe & Together Institute - 2020
- Couple Counselling – Institution: Sophia College – 2020
- NDIS Workers Orientation Module – NDIS Quality and Safeguards Commission – 2020
- Cert. COVID-19: Adapting Child Protection Case Management – Institution: University of Strathclyde and Celcis – 2020
- Cert. Kimochis®, Social and emotional tools for practicing emotional self-regulation and positive relationships – Institution: Kimochis® – 2019
- Cert. *eSafetyWomen—online training for frontline workers* – Institution: eSafety Women Commissioner – 2019
- Cert. Domestic Violence Response Training *Institution: LifeLine* – 2013 refresher training completed in 2018
- Public Speakers University – *Institution: Andy Harrington* – 2015
- Pre & Post Abortion Professional Training – *Institution: Doctors for Life* – 2001

Awards Azelene has achieved include:
- Local Heroes for Westfield Whitford City Shopping Centre Finalist 2020
- Nominated for Telstra Businesswomen's Awards 2018
- Australian Mumpreneur Award Finalist Making a Difference Non-Profit 2016
- Australian Mumpreneur Awards Finalist Big Ideas Award 2016
- Mrs Galaxy 2015 National Finalist
- Mrs Charity for Make A Wish First Runner Up 2015
- Mrs Charity for Wildlife Warriors First Place 2015
- Winner of the Nifnex Influential 100 Business Awards 2015

"Use the darkness of your past to propel you to a brighter future."
-Donata Joseph-

In the Media & Events

My journey, commitment and involvement with:
From Fear To Freedom By: Adrian Kwan

At the launce of *From Fear to Freedom* a book she and her daughter is featuring in written by: Adrian Kwan

Keynote Speaker

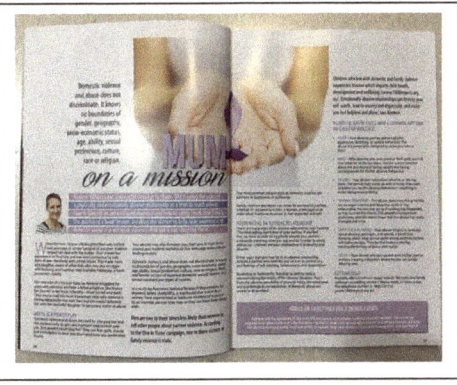

Sian Williams Founder & Azelene Williams Co-Founder of Kidzucate

"Azelene & Sian Williams are not just an ordinary mom and daughter. If the two of them put their business hats on, they are an unstoppable powerhouse who has travelled internationally as part of their passion for Human Rights. They have shared stages as motivational speakers, they have been on Today Tonight and Sunrise on Channel 7, and on Today on Channel 9, they have also appeared in numerous News Papers and Magazines across the world. Together they Advocate unconditionally against Bullying and Domestic and Family Violence."

With my husband and Sian's dad Glyn Williams who is one of our biggest supporters.

Take-A-Stand Against Bullying

When I'm not advocating against domestic violence. I advocate against bullying alongside my daughter Sian Williams, the founder of Kidzucate. I believe there is a massive connection between domestic and family violence and bullying. Teach a child positive behaviour towards others from birth and, they will most likely grow up respecting other people's feelings. Teach them anger and aggression, and they will most likely act out those behaviours in one way or another in our schools and community through Bullying. There is no excuse for any form of abuse towards another. No-one deserves to be abused. And NO child deserves to witness violence and go to bed in fear.

1000women1000ways Interview in 2016 with: Jennifer Gillson

2015 National Finalist for Mrs. Galaxy

Never **STOP** something you love to do because of someone else's issues.

Every 10 years I chop my long black hair off towards cancer awareness after my dad died of cancer in 1999.

In 2015 I found myself on the ramp again. This time as National Finalist for Mrs Galaxy Australia. I used this platform with Galaxy to advocate even more against Domestic and Family Violence.

Trip to Canberra

Being invited by the Prime Minister of Australian Malcolm Turnbull to lunch at the Lodge was one of the highlights of our trip to Canberra.

Mr Ian Goodenough was our host in Canberra and took us on a private tour through Parliament House.

Meeting with Michaelia Cash

Azelene is a My Story My Time Media Advocate for Ruah Communities. She regularly shares her story in the media in 2020 she worked alongside the Department of Justice on a new public education campaign to inform and empower West Australians about suffocation and strangulation. As part of this campaign, she was interviewed by ABC and Channel 10 on the day of the launch.

https://www.wa.gov.au/government/ announcements/new-weapons-the- fight-against-strangulation

Healthy & Respectful Relationship Blueprint

Part 2

www.azelenewilliams.com

www.kidzucate.com

azelenewilliams@gmail.com

All the research and ideas use to compile the Healthy & Respectful Relationship Blueprint in Part 2 of this book have been referenced at the end of this book. If there is any shortage of referencing a specific source, please inform the Author so that the necessary corrections can be made in a revised print.

Healthy & Respectful Relationship Blueprint

Topics

- Identify the Problems
- Identify some of the Triggers
- The Effect of Domestic Violence
- The Effect of Power & Control
- Children's Domestic Abuse Wheel
- The effect Abuse has on Children
- Circle of Violence
- Recognize-Respond-Refer
- Healthy Boundaries
- Moving Forward
- Healthy Boundaries
- Equality & Empowerment of a Healthy Relationship
- Love and Care for your Child
- Nurturing your Child
- Care for Yourself
- Wheel of Life

Identify the problem

- Physical Abuse
- Emotional Abuse
- Verbal Abuse
- Economic or Financial Abuse
- Mental or Psychological Abuse
- Sexual Abuse
- Spiritual Abuse
- Social Abuse
- Adult Bullying

What is Physical Abuse?

- Standing over you
- Getting "In your face."
- Blocking a door
- Grabbing you when you try to leave
- Kicking
- Punching
- Biting
- Slapping
- Choking
- Threatening to harm you
- Using weapons

What is Emotional Abuse?

- Insults
- Put-downs
- Intimidating you
- Embarrassing you in public
- Talking down to you
- Not listening or respecting your feelings
- Making threats
- Calling you names
- Swearing at you
- Making you feel you're not good enough
- Destroying your belongings and personal items

What is Verbal Abuse?

- Yelling
- Shouting
- Swearing
- Continuously arguing
- Interrupting
- Talking over you
- Putting you down
- Using loud and threatening language, and tone to cause fear
- Name calling
- Intimidating you
- Mocking

What is Economic Abuse?

- Withholding money or other financial benefits
- Opening up a joint account but you don't have access to the account
- Forcing you to leave your job
- Forcing you to get fired
- Shaming you for how you spend money
- Not allowing you to work or get an education and isolating you by doing that
- Putting all the accounts and credit cards in their name
- Preventing you from using a car

What is Mental Abuse?

- Playing mind games with you
- Twisting everything around so nothing is their fault and all of their behaviours was caused by something you did or didn't do
- Accusing you of doing things that they are doing
- Lying
- Manipulating you for control or sex
- Threatening to kick you out of the house
- Threatening to kill you or the kids
- Destroying reality so, you think you are losing your mind

What is Sexual Abuse?

- Rape
- Unwanted sexual touching
- Vulgar comments
- Pressure for sex
- Forcing you to get pregnant or to have an abortion
- Forcing you to have sex
- Forcing you to text sexual photos or naked photos of yourself
- Posting private pictures of you on the internet or threatening to do so

What is Spiritual Abuse?

- Denial and misuse of religious beliefs
- Practices to force victims into subordinate roles
- Misusing religion or spiritual traditions to justify physical violence or other abuse

What is Social Abuse?

- Isolation from friends and family
- Instigating and controlling relocations
- Living outside a social circle
- Controlling employment opportunities
- Not allowing you to have friends or meet people

Identify some of the triggers

- Alcohol
- Drugs
- Anger
- Cultural, religious & class differences
- Mental problems
- It might be that the enemy within the abuser stem from their upbringing
- Unhealthy beliefs (To name a few)

Activity ~
What other triggers are there in your relationship? What can you do to avoid them?

_____
_____
_____
_____
_____
_____
_____
_____
_____
_____

The effect of Domestic Violence

- Murder / Homicide
- Health impacts
- Negative impact on children
- Homelessness
- Economic Impact
- Suicide
- Depression (To name a few)

Activity ~
Identify more effects that you have experienced before.

_____
_____
_____
_____
_____
_____
_____
_____
_____
_____
_____
_____

The Effect of Power & Control

Using Intimidation

- Making you afraid by using looks, actions, gestures
- Breaking things
- Vandalising of property
- Hurting your pets
- Threatening you with weapons

Using Emotional Abuse

- Putting you down
- Making you feel bad about yourself all the time
- Name calling
- Making you feel that you are mentally unstable
- Playing mind games and confusing you
- Humiliating you in front of people
- Making you feel guilty about everything you do

Using Isolation

- Controlling what you do and where you go
- Control whom you are allowed to see and talk to
- What you watch on TV and read
- Whom you take with you when you go out
- Limiting your time in your community
- Justify their actions by making you out as jealous

Minimising, Denying and Blaming

- Making light of the abuse and telling you it is not as bad as you are making it out to be
- Denying the abuse
- Blaming you for the abusive behaviours
- Saying you cause the problem around the issues

Using Children

- When it comes to the children, you feel guilty
- Talking through the children
- Saying untrue things to the kids about you
- Threatening to hurt or take the children

Using Male & Female Privilege

- Treating and using you as a slave
- Not allowing you to make important decisions
- Acting as the "the King of the house."
- You are not allowed to define men's and women's roles
- Expecting them or you to bring in all the money
- Blaming you for not being there for the kids when they need to work
- Blaming you for their unhappy life

Using Economic Abuse

- Not allowing you to work
- Not giving you money for the home
- Giving you an allowance but make you ask for it
- Have joint accounts but, you have no access
- Not telling you what their income is per month and if there is a savings account

Using Coercion and Threats

- Threatening you with weapons and making sure you know there is a weapon
- Threatening to leave you
- Threatening to commit suicide
- Threatening to kill the children or you
- Threatening to report you for "no" reason
- Forcing you to drop charges if any
- Forcing you to do illegal things on their behalf

Abuse Effects Children

Photo Credit: Sian Williams
This is my daughter, and she is the reason why I will never stop advocating against domestic and family violence.

The effect Abuse has on children

Emotional Abuse

- Doubting things and people in their lives
- In fear of doing things wrong
- Inconsistent limits and expectations by the caregiver
- Scared to usually expressing their feelings
- Find it difficult to learn at school
- Very Low self-esteem and don't like themselves

Physical & Mental Effects

- Thinking everything is their fault, having guilt and shame because of that
- Having problems with stages of development
- Demanding and needy
- Withdrawn from people and things
- Show unhealthy physical or sexual behaviours
- Show bullying behaviours at school
- Disrespect teachers, friends and other people

Using Children

- The child ends up in the middle of a fight
- Children taking on roles and responsibilities of their parents and struggle to be a child
- Children are not allowed to voice themselves
- Children used to start or end the conflict
- Telling a child to take sides
- Disrespecting one or the other parent because of influence

Sexual Abuse

- Shy about their bodies
- Feeling threatened & fearful of their sexuality
- Adapting inappropriate sexual talk and behaviours
- Children watching pornographic material online or in magazines
- Unhealthy behaviours around exploring their bodies and showing unhealthy curiosity

Threats

- Learn to manipulate others and to threatening people around them because of what they have learned
- Exploded anger that results into violent, abusive acts
- Imploding anger and not knowing how to deal with it because of their own fears
- Not knowing how to express emotions, cry, show empathy and sympathy
- Fearing to say when they have wet their bed
- Not going to get food to eat

Sexual Stereotyping

- Copying dominant and abusive behaviours
- Being ashamed of themselves
- Unable to express their feelings

Intimidation

- Putting children in fear by:
    - Using scary or angry looks
    - Loud actions
    - Big gestures
    - Shouting and using loud voices
    - Throwing and smashing things
    - Destroying or breaking property
- Unsure of physical and emotional safety
- Turn out as a child with Bully behaviours

Isolation

- Lack of developing social skills
- Feeling cut off from friends, alone and different
- Violence is not allowing them to bring friends home
- Being forced to keep "secrets"
- Losing trust in adults and people who are supposed to care for them

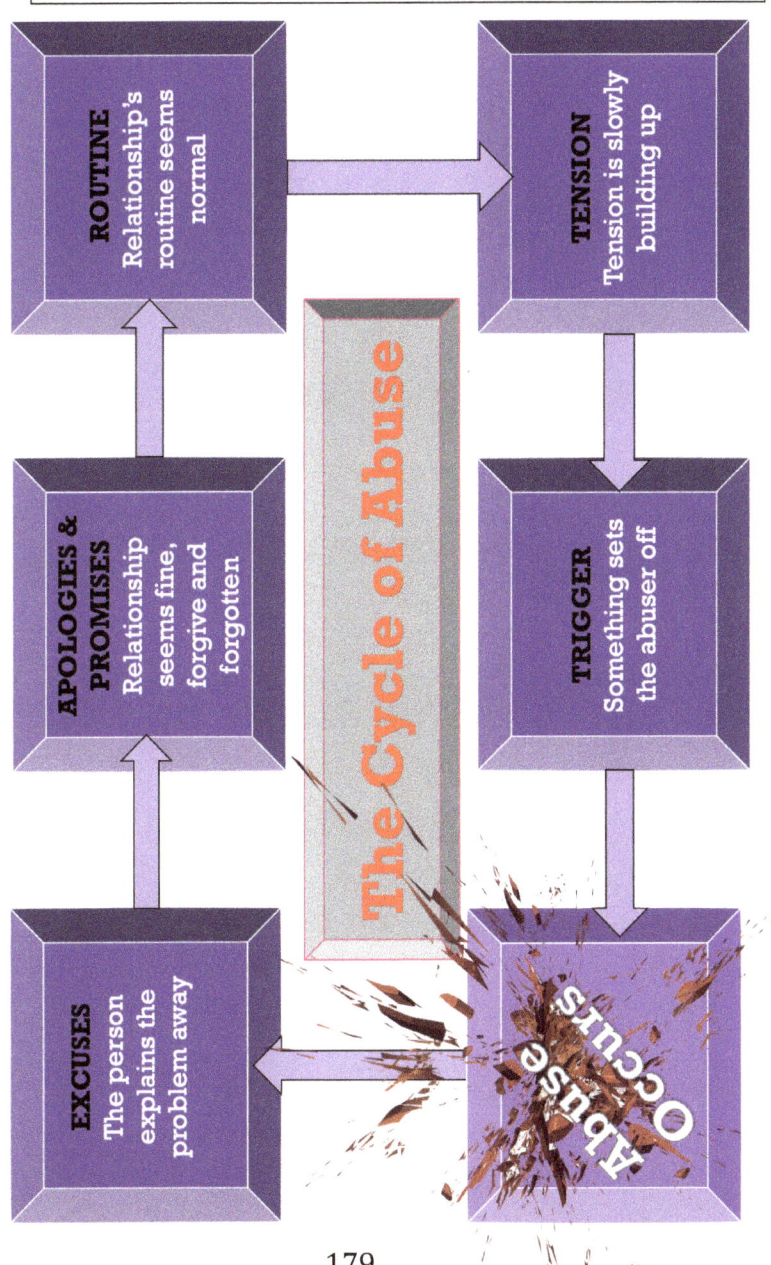

To STOP Domestic Violence is everyone's responsibility! This is what you can do to help:

Recognise the signs of Domestic Violence

Respond by listening when someone tells you they are being abused. Believe them!

Record by making notes of what was said and what happened

Report to the Police, Department of Communities – Child Protection and Family Support or another organisation.

OR

Refer to the Lifeline, 1800Respect, RUAH Community Services or similar organisations

For Help in Australia Contact:

RUAH Community Services: 13 RUAH (13 78 24)
1800RESPECT: 1800 737 732
Child Protection and Family Support: 08 9222 2555
Kids Helpline: 1800 551 800
Lifeline: 13 11 14
Police: 131 444
Anglicare: 1300 11 44 46
Patricia Giles: 08 9300 0340
Women's Council: 08 9420 7264

Healthy Boundaries

What do they do, and why do we need them?

- Boundaries are physical, emotional, sexual and mental limits we set in relationships that protect us from being controlled, manipulated, abused, or exploited.
- They make it possible for us to separate our own thoughts and feelings from those of others and to take responsibility for what we think, feel and do.
- They make it possible for us to accept "No" from others and to say "No" ourselves.
- They make it possible to be aware of where you end, and another begins.
- They enable us to make choices about how we feel, think or behave.
- They help draw a line between "me" and "you".

Healthy Boundaries

- A person with healthy boundaries can identify:
    - How he or she feels about something
    - What he or she thinks about something
    - How to react
    - How to behave in situations

- A person with healthy boundaries can distinguish between his or her own emotions, opinions, and behaviours and those of others
- A person with healthy boundaries takes responsibility for his or her actions
- A person with healthy boundaries does not blame others for how he or she thinks, feels and behaves
- A person with healthy boundaries does not allow a person with unhealthy boundaries to control them; they stand up for themselves and others
- A person with healthy boundaries can say "No" when their boundaries are intruded upon and will act on a person that would not respect that in a sensible way
- A person with healthy boundaries is honest, responsible, open and trustworthy

Activity ~

Make a list of Healthy Boundaries you might be able to use.

_____
_____
_____
_____

Some Healthy Boundaries to help you set your own.

- Ability to adapt and change when it is needed and appropriate
- Do not overreact to what is happening around them
- Able to say "No" when it is appropriate
- Able to accept constructive criticism or feedback without personalising it
- Able to accept "No" from others without taking it personally
- Able to stand up for themselves
- Know how they feel, what they think and how they behave
- Take responsibility for meeting their own needs
- Take responsibility for their emotions, their ideas and their behaviour
- Making decisions not just for themselves but their entire family

List additional healthy boundaries you can put in place:
_____
_____
_____
_____
_____
_____
_____
_____
_____
_____

Equality & Empowerment of a Healthy Relationship

Non-Threatening Behaviours

- You are safe and comfortable being around the person in your life
- Enjoying life and expressing yourself is never a problem in the relationship

Respect

- Not getting judged when you say things
- Being emotionally supported
- Your opinions matter in the relationship

Trust and Support

- Supporting what you would like to accomplish in life
- Respecting your friends, your personal boundaries and who you are

Honesty & Accountability

- Accepting responsibility for their actions
- Acknowledging mistakes and when wrong
- Admitting when they were abusive
- Being honesty through communication and actions

Responsible Parenting

- Sharing responsibilities as a parent
- Respectful parents and being a good role model for their children

Shared Responsibility

- Sharing day to day activities and responsibilities
- Making decisions as a family and talking about things if opinions and feelings are different

Economic Partnership

- Share money responsibilities
- Financial arrangements are not one-sided both partners are equal
- Family money is family money it's there for the entire family to use

Negotiation and being Fair

- Resolving conflict in a positive way where both parties are satisfied with the outcome
- Open towards new ideas and changes
- Sometimes compromising their own needs

Nurturing Your Children

Promote Emotional Security

- Allowing a child to express what they feel. Teach them it is normal to have feelings such as sad, happy, angry, fear and more
- Being there when your child needs you
- Being caring, supportive and give unconditional love to your children

Provide Physical Security

- Provide basic needs such as food, home, and clothing
- Teach your child personal hygiene & nutrition
- Responsible for their safety:
    - On social media
    - Where they go and with whom
    - What they watch on TV
    - Who they are friends with
- Provide a safe family home and space to grow
- Give medical attention when they need it

Provide Discipline

- Be consistent about rules and morels
- Rules should be age appropriate and in line with their development stage
- Be clear on what you expect of your children
- Use discipline to change negative habits

Give Time

- Be involved in your children's lives: Activities, School, Sports, Special Events, Celebrations, Friends
- Invite your children to join your activities. Take them with you to child-appropriate events
- Share who you are with your children. Assure them that you have made mistakes yourself when growing up.

Support & Encourage

- Be affirming
- Encourage children to follow their dreams
- Let your children disagree with you and allow family debates
- When a child improves tell them
- Teach your child life skills
- Teach them tools to help them through their lives
- Allow your children to make mistakes and encourage them to learn out of it

Give Affection

- Express your love with hugs and kind words
- Don't be afraid to support your child when they are physically or emotionally hurt show them you care

Care for Yourself

- Give yourself personal time
- Keep yourself healthy
- Maintain friendships
- Accept love

Trust & Respect

- Acknowledge children's rights to have their own feelings, opinions, friends and activities
- Promote independence
- Allow for privacy
- Respect their feelings for another parent
- Believe your children
- Don't offer to help but assure that you are there when they need help

Physical self-care

- Eat regularly & healthy
- Get medical care when needed
- Colour your hair
- Cut your hair
- Make sure to get enough sleep
- Wear clothes and colours, you love
- Take time away from the phone
- Work out
- Take time off when needed
- Go for a relaxing massage
- Go for reflexology

- Do physical in and outdoor activities
- Be intimate with yourself
- Take a holiday
- Go camping

Psychological self-care

- Say "No" to extra responsibilities sometimes
- Practice receiving from others and not always giving
- Trying new things can be exciting: art, auctions, theatre
- Listen to your inner needs. Not just thoughts but feelings as well
- Let others know different aspects of you
- Decrease stress in your life
- Do something where you are not an expert or in charge
- Read literature that is unrelated to work
- Write in a journal
- Go for counselling
- Make time for self-reflection
- Be curious

Emotional self-care

- Spend time with others whose company you enjoy
- Stay in contact with important people in your life
- Give yourself affirmation and praise yourself
- Find things to laugh about
- It's ok to cry

- Do something nice for somebody else
- Love yourself for who you are
- Read favourite books
- Watch favourite movies
- Identify fun stuff
- Meditate
- Keep a journal
- Visit a good friend
- Meet new, like-minded people

Spiritual self-care

- Make time for meditation & reflection
- Spend time in nature
- Participate in a gathering - community group that has meaning
- Be open to inspiration
- Cherish your optimism & hope
- Be aware of non-tangible (non-material) aspects of life
- Be open to mystery, not knowing
- Identify what is meaningful to you & notice its place in your life

Workplace / Professional Self-Care

- Take time to eat lunch
- Take time to chat with co-workers
- Make time to complete tasks
- Identify projects or tasks that are exciting, growth-promoting & rewarding for you
- Set limits with clients & colleagues

- Balance your caseload, so no one day is too much!
- Arrange your workspace, so it is comfortable & comforting
- Negotiate for your needs (benefits, pay rise)
- Have a peer / collegial support group

Wheel of Life Example:

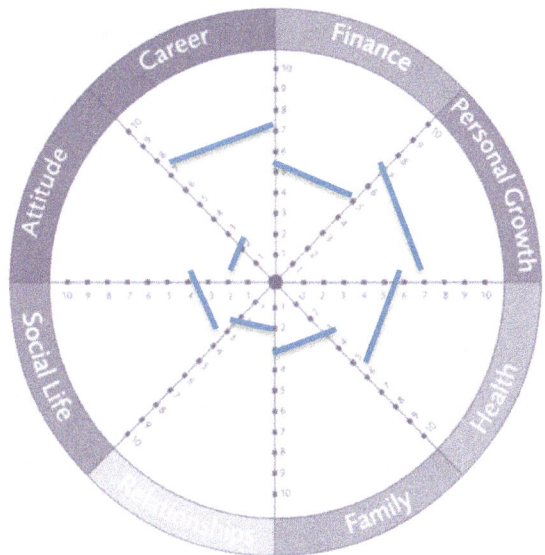

On a scale from 0 to 10, what does your life look like?

Review your wheel every 6 to 12 months.

The objective is to get a balance in your life.

You do not have to get to a scale of 10; it is more important to have a balance then focusing on reaching 10.

Azelene Williams
FROM FEAR TO FREEDOM

Wheel of Life

Name: _____ Start Date: _____

MY LIFE SCORE OUT OF 10
BAD ~ 0   1   2   3   4   5   6   7   8   9   10 ~ GOOD

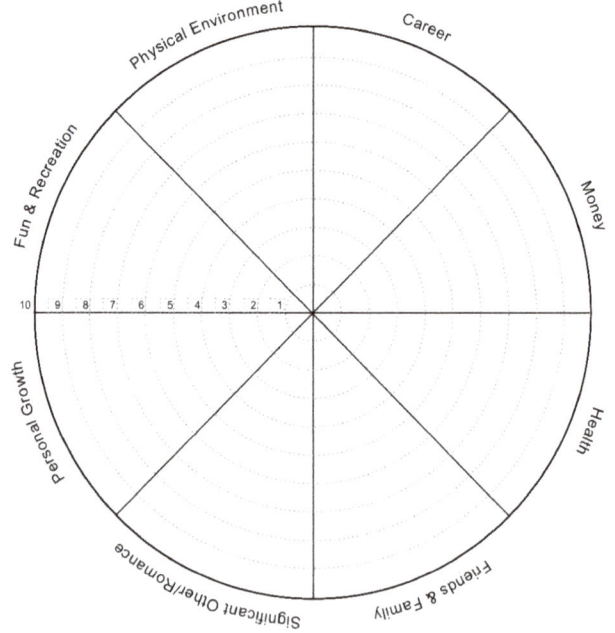

DO A NEW ENTRY EVERY 6 MONTHS

Reflecting on my own life:

What does my relationship look like?

_____
_____
_____
_____
_____
_____

What is making me happy in my relationship?

_____
_____
_____
_____
_____
_____
_____

What is making me unhappy in my relationship?

_____
_____
_____
_____
_____
_____
_____

How can I change this and what boundaries should I put in place?

_____
_____
_____

Acknowledgements

Glyn Williams:

Our marriage has had its ups and downs, but I want to thank you for being my friend, my husband and my biggest support system throughout our journey together. When things are tough we don't just leave it hanging. We talk about it and if it's too close for comfort we have never been scared to get professional help to help us work through our issues. I think this is what I appreciate about you. We are not scared to make positive changes and build stronger foundations for our family and us to grow as a couple. I love you more than anything else and hope to grow very old with you.

Sian Hunter Williams:

You are the love of my life. I thank God for giving you to me. Sian, please be open minded and enjoy your life, but look out for things that don't feel right. If you believe there is something going on, listen to that inner voice. Promise me you will speak up when you are in trouble and when you need help. You don't have to talk to me, but at least talk to someone you can trust and who is responsible enough to help and guide you. I love you more than anything in this world. I believe you will live a happy life. Learn from your mistakes and always look for the positive when times are dark.

Remember, we all have choices in life. If you make the wrong ones don't go and blame others for it. Look at the choices you made and don't make the same mistakes over and over again. Life is great, but life can sometimes suck! Remember it's ok to get angry but think of the consequences and repercussions. Sian, I believe in healthy ways and interesting techniques to get rid of anger, and to cope when you experience challenges. I have taught you to use some of these techniques and ways to express your anger in a safe and healthy way from a very young age.

Keep on using those tools, they might just help you one day when you need them most.

Joan Riekert:
Mom, thanks for your love throughout my life. I am sorry that life didn't always treat you as well as it should have. But I have learned a lot from you and I appreciate the space you gave me when I needed it the most. You were always there to catch me and to support me if I needed help. I love you very much.

Ronell Riekert:
We have seen each other happy, sad and hurt. We have had our issues in life but always seemed to sort it out in a good way in the end. Everything we went through made us stronger. Thank you for being there when I needed you the most. I love you and will always have a special place for you in my heart. You are the best sister in the world.

Elzette Grobler-Brits:
You were the first friend who opened a door and heart for me, after Paul and I broke up. You were living in the flat around the corner from mine and I will never forget the day I knocked on your door to say, "Please keep an ear open if I scream for help." You invited me in and a long friendship was the result of that first meeting. Thank you for your support, your love and your shoulder when I needed a friend and after I lost all my friends☺

Hannes Riekert:
My Dad, passed away in 1999
"I love you Dad, and I miss you very much!"
There is so much that I would like to share with you. The good and the bad! If I had one wish I would have wished to spend the day with you!

Paul:
You tried hard to break me; you even tried to kill me - more than once. You have not succeeded, and I thank God for that!

Chantal Swanepoel:
For giving me the idea to put my book down in public spaces for people to find.

Justine O'Malley:
Who believed in me and motivated me to enroll in a Degree in Social Work. Who gave me numerous opportunities to deliver workshops, programs and telling my story in schools and in the community. You will never know how much I appreciate and respect your guidance and friendship!

The Media:
Who helped and supported myself and Sian's dream over the years to make the world a better place. We wouldn't have had the exposure if it wasn't for the media's support.

PHOTO GALLARY

In Memory of my Dad
Hannes Riekert 1934 to 1999

In Memory of my Modeling Mentor
Peter van Eck

I was at my happiest when I was on the runway. These photos were part of the collection that was used at the modeling showcase were Paul was so disgusted with my performance and the photos that were showcased on the big screen.

The top two photos were the end of my modeling career. Paul was in a rage of anger while they showcased them on stage on evening as part of the modelling show I participated in.

My young love story that almost cost me my life.

 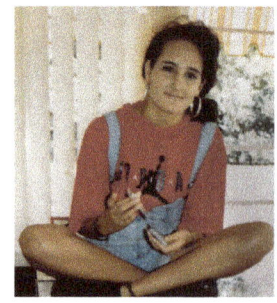

Azelene and Paul in the first year of their relationship.

> **Life is full of challenges.
> In the end, it's getting up that pulls us through
> the dark, painful days.**
> ~Azelene Williams~

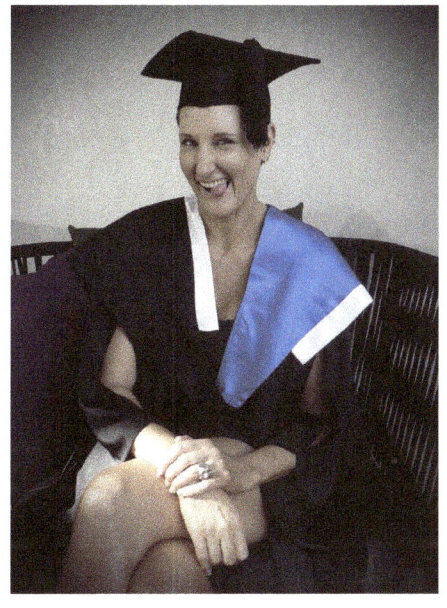

**Azelene Williams graduated with a
Bachelor of Social Work
during the COVID-19 in 2020 with dyslexia.**

"Today I am the advocate, mentor, registered counsellor and social worker I needed when I was a teenager."

Resources in Australia:

From Fear to Freedom
https://www.azelenewilliams.com
WA Child Safety Services
https://wachildsafetyservices.com/
Women's Council:
http://www.womenscouncil.com.au/womens-refuges.html
1800RESPECT:
https://www.1800respect.org.au/
RUAH Community Services
https://www.ruah.org.au/
Helping Minds:
https://helpingminds.org.au/
Black Dog Institute
https://www.blackdoginstitute.org.au/clinical-resources/suicide-self-harm/warning-signs
Western Australia Police Force – Report DV
https://www.police.wa.gov.au/Your-Safety/Family-and-domestic-violence
Reach out.com
https://au.reachout.com/tough-times/abuse-and-violence?gclid=CjwKCAiAqbvTBRAPEiwANEkyCCBxVsA7Zaf944L8vBBIpTJmsOcGTQIld40Y1HUbZwrFSPi4gR5nlhoCPKwQAvD_BwE
DV-alert Domestic Violence Response Training
http://www.dvalert.org.au/what-we-offer/what-offer
Headspace
https://headspace.org.au/
No Limits Perth
https://www.nolimitsperth.org.au/

BROKEN
Breaking the Silence

By: Azelene Williams

www.azelenewilliams.com
www.kidzucate.com

FROM FEAR TO FREEDOM

ISBN 978-0-646-98390-5

References

Did You Know - Change Is Possible (CHIPS) Family Violence Shelter. (n.d.). Retrieved from http://www.chipsfvs.org/did-you-know.html

Invisible Kinds Of Abuse | Rouge Lioness. (n.d.). Retrieved from
http://rougelioness.org/2015/01/invisible-kinds-of-abuse/

Abuse Characteristics | Healing Hearts and Families. (n.d.). Retrieved from http://healingheartsandfamilies.com/abuse-characteristics/

Do Controlled Women Ever Really Break Away? - Find Answers to ... (n.d.). Retrieved from
http://www.experienceproject.com/question-answer/Do-Controlled-Women-Ever-Really

Unhealthy Relationship's Characteristics. (n.d.). Retrieved from
http://charmeck.org/city/charlotte/CMPD/organization/investigative/SpecialVictim

City of Knoxville - Domestic Violence Tests. (n.d.). Retrieved from http://www.cityofknoxville.org/kpd/dvu_test.asp

AMAredoeffects on child. (n.d.). Retrieved from
http://cmtfbw.org/AMAredoeffectsonchild.html

Children's Domestic Abuse Wheel - Home | Child Matters. (n.d.). Retrieved from
http://www.childmatters.org.nz/file/Diploma-Readings/Block-2/Family-Violence/6.1

Violence Affects Children and Nurturing Helps to Heal Poster. (n.d.). Retrieved from
http://www.peelregion.ca/health/professionals/ask/pdf/violence.pdf

FGUA, What Do They Do And Why Do We Pay? | lehighacresgazette ... (n.d.). Retrieved from
http://lehighacresgazette.info/news/fgua-what-do-they-do-and-why-do-we-pay/

Why Healthy Boundaries are Important in Relationships ... (n.d.). Retrieved from
http://www.kellevision.com/kellevision/2009/12/boundaries-schmoundares.html

What are boundaries and are they biblical? - GotQuestions.org. (n.d.). Retrieved from
http://www.gotquestions.org/boundaries-biblical.html

Why Healthy Boundaries are Important in Relationships ... (n.d.). Retrieved from
http://www.kellevision.com/kellevision/2009/12/boundaries-schmoundares.html

Boundaries - Addiction Consulting.com. (n.d.). Retrieved from http://www.addictionconsulting.com/boundaries.htm

Why Healthy Boundaries are Important in Relationships ... (n.d.). Retrieved from
http://www.kellevision.com/kellevision/2009/12/boundaries-schmoundares.html

THE ABUSE OF CHILDREN WHEEL - LFCC. (n.d.). Retrieved from http://www.lfcc.on.ca/HCT_SWASM_pages22-23.pdf

Core Competencies: Peer Role: Self Care SELF-ASSESSMENT TOOL ... (n.d.). Retrieved from
http://peer.hdwg.org/sites/default/files/7b%20SelfAssessmentToolSelfCare-PeerRol

Take home Self-care Assessment Tool. (n.d.). Retrieved from
http://www.actassupport.com.au/pdf/SelfCareAssessmentTool.pdf

Organizational Self-Care Assessment. (n.d.). Retrieved from
http://www.familyhomelessness.org/media/95.pdf

Domestic abuse intervention programs. (n.d.). Retrieved from
https://www.theduluthmodel.org/

All the research and ideas use to compile the Healthy & Respectful Relationship Blueprint in Part 2 of this book have been referenced at the end of this book. If there is any shortage of referencing a specific source, please inform the Author so that the necessary corrections can be made in a revised print.

www.ingramcontent.com/pod-product-compliance
Lightning Source LLC
Chambersburg PA
CBHW062109290426
44110CB00023B/2758